Spiritual Guide To Our Health

ULLA SARMIENTO

Ulla Sarmiento, DVM, PhD

Spiritual Guide To Our Health

ISBN: 9798431444135

DISCLAIMER

The health and disease information in this book is provided as an information resource only, and is not to be used or relied upon for any diagnostic or treatment purposes. Please consult your healthcare provider before making any healthcare decisions about your condition. The author is not engaged in rendering medical advice or services. Accordingly, the author disclaims any liability, loss, damage or injury caused by the use or application of contents of this work. No warranty, express or implied, is delivered by the author with respect to the contents of this work.

BIG PICTURE QUESTIONS - Book 6

Bridging Science and Spirituality

Book Series:

Spiritual Guide To Our Multiverse - Book 1

Guía Espiritual a Nuestro Multiverso - Book 1 (Spanish)

Spiritual Guide To Our Afterlife - Book 2

Spiritual Guide To Our Relationships - Book 3

Spiritual Guide To Our Universal Laws - Book 4

Spiritual Guide To Our Awakening - Book 5

TABLE OF CONTENTS

INTRODUCTION

Are you ready to find out who you are and why you are here? How is your body animated? How is the body created? What causes dis-ease or disease in our physical form? What is the energetic basis of physical and mental conditions that afflict people? What can we do about it? How do we balance western medicine and energy medicine approaches to heal ourselves?

If you have been wondering about these questions, then come along, because I wrote this book to give you a jumpstart into new ways of looking at the basis of our health, well-being and disease that profoundly affect how we operate here as incarnate entities.

You can read more about the greater reality in my first book ("Spiritual Guide To Our Multiverse") published in 2018. You can find out more about death and the afterlife in my second book ("Spiritual Guide To Our Afterlife") published in 2019. You can also learn more about yourself in relationships with other people in my third book ("Spiritual Guide To Our Relationships") published in 2020. This book has more spiritual science than ever.

My fourth book ("Spiritual Guide To Our Universal Laws") explains the laws and sub-laws governing our life using modern spiritual science instead of ancient mumbo jumbo. My fifth book puts it all together to see the Big Picture for awakening ourselves and humanity as a whole ("Spiritual Guide To Our Awakening"). This is the sixth book in the Big Picture Questions series on the topic of Health and Healing.

I am a research scientist turned into a spiritual scientist and my goal is to bridge spirituality and science, to demystify spirituality, to see it as the higher frequency science it is with states of "beingness" that are part of the energetic continuum, not something that can't be mixed.

Scientists like to study the material world and spiritual scientists study the energetic world that includes and goes beyond the physical world. That's the Big Picture.

I spent the first part of my life learning all about animals and their disease conditions, looking down a microscope and studying tissues and cells to figure out how various conditions affect our physical bodies. Then I wanted to go even deeper, so I learned to clone and sequence genes and map them onto chromosomes. What I discovered was a fascinating micro-universe operating within all living beings. That was just the beginning.

There are "fractal" patterns that are self-similar and repeated all over nature, just as the second Hermetic Principle states: "As above, so below; as below, so above."

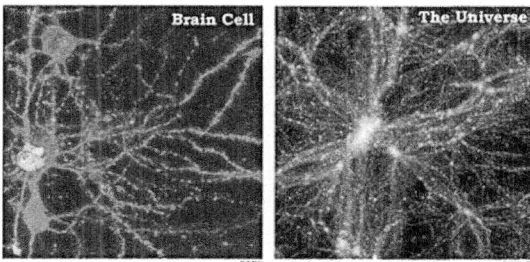

I spent the next part of my life looking up from the microscope to see the bigger picture. I used my research skills to gather, discern and assimilate information from many sources. I began to ask age-old questions and summarized the answers in my blog with over 590+ posts thusfar (BigPictureQuestions.com).

In the process, I read hundreds of books and articles and

listened to countless interviews, channels and workshops. I learned to sense subtle energies within and all around us. I honed my intuitive skills and learned to connect with my Higher Self and Source and Origin for guidance.

What I came to realize is that there is much more to us than what we can see with a microscope or a telescope. The word "spiritual" simply refers to higher frequencies holding energies in forms that most people can't perceive. The truth is simple.

"Energy is everything and that's all there is to it." — *Albert Einstein*

In this book, my goal is to share some Big Picture concepts about our human journey, which is to take care of our physical form, so we can experience, learn and evolve in it for as long as our soul wants to stay incarnate. Once we learn to do that, we can operate at a new level in life and beyond.

This book is meant to blow your old mindset away. Spirituality is no longer a mystery. We can understand both science and spirituality in their real terms, not couched in scientific misconceptions or spiritual or religious myths. Let the journey of a thousand epiphanies begin!

Disclaimer: *The health and medical information in this book is provided as an information resource only, and is not to be used or relied on for any diagnostic or treatment purposes. Please consult your health care provider before making any health care decisions about your condition. I am simply a messenger communicating new information to others, not a healer or a therapist.*

"Nothing in life is to be feared, it is only to be understood. Now is the time to understand more, so that we may fear less." — *Marie Curie*

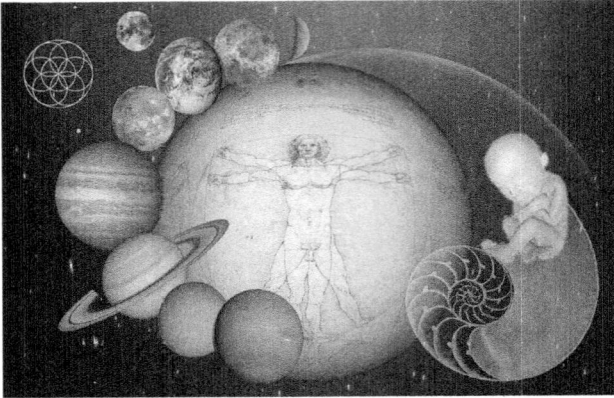

CHAPTER 1

WHERE DO WE COME FROM?

"Life is eternal and there is only One of Us."
— Neale Donald Walsch

Here is the Big Picture given in my previous books for some context on how and why we are here as human beings on Earth. Life has an agenda, which is to experience, learn and evolve.

In my first book ("Spiritual Guide To Our Multiverse") we learned that our **Source** (or God) created billions of **Higher Selves** that are Mini-Me's or smaller individualized units of itself. That's who we really are. We are sentient entities, just like Source, only smaller.

The next thing our Source created was a playground for us to explore, which is a *multiverse* (or multiple universes). Our job is to help our Source evolve by going from the bottom to the top of the multiverse. In so doing, we experience, learn and evolve from everything we encounter in every single universe — not just in passing but in minute detail. Right now we are in the *physical universe* at the bottom of the multiverse. Since our Higher Selves are too big to go there (below), they have to send Mini-Me's or smaller aspects of themselves called **souls** to incarnate there. That's your true "Selfie" right there!

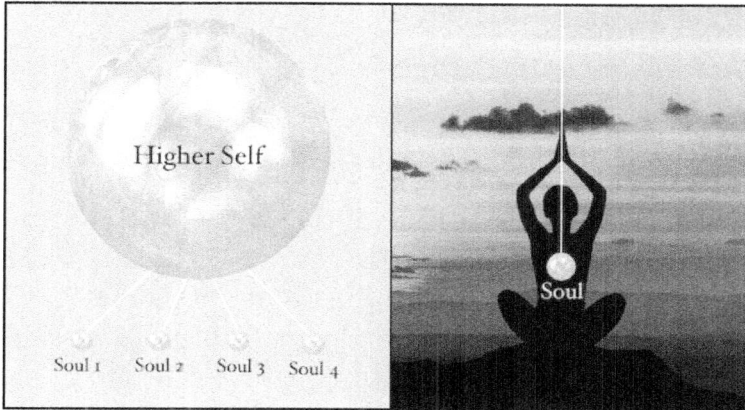

Think of the *soul* as the **driver** and the *physical body* as the **car** that the soul drives around for a lifetime (below). The soul needs a vehicle or a body to embody spirit safely into form. But don't confuse yourself with the car you drive. You are not the body or even the soul, because you are that much bigger entity called the Higher Self.

Why do we incarnate? Our Higher Selves are *creator entities* in training. They are in charge of the incarnation program that takes place in the physical universe. They thought it would be a fun game to dip into a lower frequency environment (like a planet or nebula), wear blinders and forget everything and then see if they could get out of it. Sounds hard, but it turns out they can!

When the Higher Selves realized that they could *evolve faster* that way, billions of them want to play that game now. They have to queue up to get the opportunity to incarnate, which is a great privilege. They have to justify why they should be allowed to evolve through incarnation.

How do we incarnate? Each Higher Self can send up to twelve *souls* to incarnate at the same time. The souls create some *karma* (or energetic links) to lower frequency thoughts, behaviors, actions and sensations, because it's very easy to become attracted or addicted to things like food, sex, alcohol, drugs, materialism, status seeking, victim mentality, etc. at this frequency level.

That puts our soul into the *karmic cycle*. The karmic links act like an anchor to pull us lower and keep us from going higher. Those links also put our Higher Self in stasis. It can't move ahead either. It's like having your feet stuck in molasses, which creates *evolutionary tension*.

But when all karma has been dissolved by all the souls, then the Higher Self jumps ahead (like a spring-loaded toy) and goes way past all the Higher Selves that never dared to incarnate. This *evolutionary jump* is the real reason why so many Higher Selves want to incarnate here.

The other reason is that some things can only be learned through incarnation. You have to *be* here to experience things firsthand, to be the actor in the movie, not just a couch potato watching the movie. Many people don't realize that incarnation is a real gift, not a curse. There are way more souls that want to incarnate than there are physical bodies to use. Bodies are quite a rare commodity. Why? Because each planet or location can only support a certain number of bodies with the resources it has. Consider yourself lucky to be here! This is the golden ticket.

Why do we come to Earth? Earth is a very special place to incarnate for several reasons. It is the most *biodiverse* planet in the whole universe. It hosts a multitude of species as flora, fauna, mineral and other types of entities that we can interact with. There's no place like it!

It is also called the *"planet of emotions,"* because here we can experience a wider emotional range (from highs to lows) than anywhere else. That makes human lifetimes more challenging, but it also makes our souls evolve faster. Why? Because we have so many different states of "beingness" to play with — not just black and white but all the shades of grey in between. We can compare and contrast all those states and learn from all of them on this special planet.

But the most important reason to come to Earth is to experience *individualized free will*. This is the only place in the universe where we are allowed to make decisions on our own. We don't have to consider others, what their needs are or how our choices will impact them.

We can be totally selfish and oblivious to others — at least for a while, until we mature and learn that the selfish way is not the best way to go forward. That's why we are being quarantined on the Earth, which is in a remote area within the Milky Way galaxy, which is in a remote location within the universe as well. We are allowed to evolve without interference from others. Otherwise, the individualized free will experiment is shot! We won't know if it works or not, if others interfere.

All other universal races have *collective free will*. That means they make decisions together as a group, because they're always connected to each other. They are learning about *collective responsibility* for their own civilization or group. Here are a few words from Source:

"You come from me, Source, and everything else comes from me, too. Your work is essential to the advancement of other races within the physical universe, since you are the pioneers of individualized free will. You are the way-showers on how to use it appropriately, effectively and efficiently. As you are learning, other races are learning, and I am learning, too. Understand the interconnectedness of everything — you, me, everyone you encounter and honor that in all."— Source (via Ulla)

What are we learning? The game we play is very different, because we look at all issues from the individual's perspective. We have to make our decisions on our own, which allows us to learn about *self-responsibility*. Our choices have consequences — we have to deal with those consequences and be accountable for our thoughts, behaviors and actions, no matter where they lead us. In the process, we learn what works and what doesn't work so well. Source explained:

"Free will is something else. It is given to humans, because it accelerates my learning and evolution as well. In effect, you multiply the amount of learning that is possible. Imagine one being vs. 1000 beings doing things individually vs. deciding things as a group. The members of the group may sense themselves as individual

consciousness, but make collective decisions. They don't have to take responsibility for their own actions. There is no self-responsibility.

That is a big part of learning, because eventually you will become Source Entities in your own right. At that point you need to know what is self-directed creativity and learning, and how to function as a unit, not just as a collective." — *Source (via Ulla)*

There are no mistakes or errors, there are just different lines of discovery for souls to explore. We are always on track, so make no comparisons, judgments or complaints about others. But if a person can resolve karma at a lower frequency level, then their soul is free of that level and can move on to explore higher levels. That makes our *ascension* out of this universe faster.

Are we doing this work alone? Believe it or not, we are never alone in any sense of the word. The Higher Self experiences everything the soul experiences, as it happens *in real time.*

We are being guided by countless other entities, including our Higher Self, our primary guide (which is another Higher Self) and dozens of different helpers (which are other souls). All these nonphysical or energetic entities help us with various aspects of our material and spiritual life from conception to birth to death and the afterlife (as described in "Spiritual Guide To Our Afterlife"). We need all the help we can get when we're on the Earth. Why?

We're scratching the bottom of the multiverse here at the densest levels of physicality. It's not easy to be in human form. We lose almost all of our connectivity to our Higher Self. We think we're totally separate and isolated from others. We feel abandoned, alone and want to connect with all kinds of people on the Earth to compensate for our poor vertical connection to our Higher Self and Source. That's part of the game here.

But we're *never* really disconnected from our Higher Self or Source. If we were disconnected, we would be dead or lifeless — our body wouldn't be animated by any spirit (sentience). That means there are no "soulless humans" among us, no matter how they behave. Meanwhile, the Higher Selves will keep working their way up the multiverse structure until all of them have experienced all the universes. There is no hierarchy here, because they are all going to the same destination (back to Source), just taking different routes to get there.

What's the point? All paths are valid from our Source's point of view. The more diverse the paths, the merrier Source is, because it evolves from everything we experience — that's our *evolutionary content*. Later when all of us reunite with Source, the multiverse cycle is over.

Then we start a NEW cycle in a new location and so it goes. Think of it as eternal job security or eternal creative play, if you prefer. Either way you're here to keep going and going.

"God is a process, not the result of that process, but the process itself. The process of creation is never complete, never done. And you are part of that process." — *Neale Donald Walsch*

CHAPTER 2

HOW DOES SPIRIT ANIMATE THE BODY?

Our Higher Self is a sentient entity that is living much higher up in the multiverse than the human being here on Earth. The Higher Self can project just one **soul** or up to twelve souls at the same time to explore different parts of the physical universe. Here is an image analogy of a Higher Self that has sent four souls outside of itself to explore different locations (below).

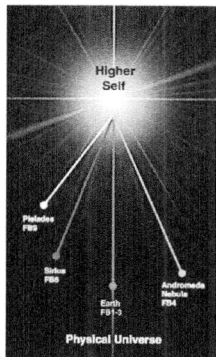

For example, it could send one soul to Earth at frequency bands 1-3 (FB 1-3), a second soul to the

Andromeda Nebula at FB 4, a third soul to Sirius at FB 6, a fourth soul to Pleiades at FB 9.

All these souls are incarnated as **different species** with different physical forms and different lifespans in different environments at different frequency levels. They all contribute to the Higher Self's overall evolution as a creator entity in training. That's why you're here!

How does a soul plan a human incarnation? The Higher Self makes the *overall life plan* and decides **which soul** and **which species** to use to carry out the plan. Then the designated soul does a lot of planning with its **guide** and **helpers**, who need to orchestrate all the planned events and logistics of meeting other souls at the right time in the right place. We don't come here just for our own evolution. We come here to *interact* with many other souls, because we all learn from working with each other (see "Spiritual Guide To Our Relationships").

The most important choice that the soul makes is **which body** to use. Using the Akashic records, the soul looks at all the potential human bodies in different locations (not just Earth). It looks at the potential parents, siblings, personalities, health and longevity of the body, friends, and other opportunities for education, career, service work, etc.

The soul also chooses what challenges, illnesses or hardships it will encounter (e.g. mental or physical disabilities, death of a loved one, divorce, accident, poverty, pandemic, migration, etc.). All this is chosen prior to being born. That's why it's a massive planning process involving many entities on the energetic side, including the incoming soul, both parents' souls and all of their guides and helpers.

The parents create the gross physical body through procreation followed by gestation from the zygote to embryo to fetus stage. But to get things started, the physical form needs a basic *energy system*, which is created and inserted into the zygote by the soul with its guide and helpers. This creates the *interface* between the soul and the dense physical matter that the soul animates.

Without the energy system in place, the zygote, embryo or fetus cannot grow. If the energy system is removed before birth, the physical form dies, and the soul goes back to the energetic side. Some souls have *planned* to experience only a short lifespan (e.g. early embryonic death, miscarriage, stillbirth, crib death, etc.). All is choice at the soul level.

How does the soul enter the body? The human vehicle is the most difficult one to work with in the entire universe. Why? It is the most addictive and complicated vehicle for a soul to use.

To ensoul a human form, the soul has to descend about a hundred levels from its Higher Self to the bottom of the multiverse. Imagine the Higher Self as a big sun and the soul as a tiny balloon next to it. The tiny balloon has to squeeze itself into a small energy vortex or tube to slide down towards the human figure on the ground (below).

The tube is called the **Hara line**, which protects the *sentient energies* of the **soul**, as it comes down the ladder of frequencies. The tube gets stretched and thinned out by the time it reaches the human figure and as a result, the communicative "bandwidth" gets reduced on the way down. It's like going from five million channels at the Higher Self level to just five channels or five senses at the human level. The connection also becomes very slow — like a dial up instead of a high-speed internet connection. That's why we lose about 99% of our connectivity with our Higher Self in human form.

The Hara line runs vertically from the Higher Self to the physical body to create a central channel that splits in the belly to go down each leg to anchor us to the Earth (closeup, below).

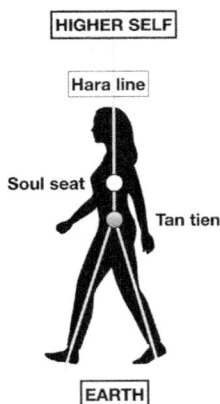

The soul's *sentience* stays at the **Soul seat** in the chest area (midline behind the sternum). It is the command center for our soul. But the soul's *energies* move down to the abdomen to a point called the **Tan tien** (above). From there the energies get distributed throughout the body via an energetic network made of major, minor and mini-chakras and energy veins that run next to the blood vessels and nerves found in the body. This is how we animate the whole body.

By the way, when the soul enters a baby's body, they sleep a lot while their physical and etheric bodies are being built. They have wide open crown chakras in the head, where the soul can enter and leave the baby's body at will. Their major chakras are still open, underdeveloped and vulnerable. That's why young children need their parent's or caretaker's aura for protection.

We do the same thing every night, when we are sleeping. Our physical body is resting and recuperating, as the soul puts the body on "automatic pilot" — it leaves just enough sentient energy to run the body's physiologic functions, while the soul goes *out of body* at night to explore or play other roles in the astral levels or higher. It comes back to the body in the morning, when you wake up and remember dreaming (or not). You may feel the soul entering back into the body, if you are clairsentient or aware and sensitive to subtle energy changes.

Note that the soul does not *permanently* enter the body at conception or at the embryonic, fetal or newborn stage, because it can and wants to move in and out of the body until the age of 4. After that the soul starts to become more connected to the body, but it's not fully integrated with the human vehicle until age 7, according to Guy Needler ("The Anne Dialogues").

What is the human form made of? We live in a sea of energy both within and without. The physical universe is created from twelve frequency bands (FB 1-12). We live in the bottom three levels (FB 1-3), but our human vehicle interfaces with ten of those levels (at FB 1-10). It is designed to fully experience the environment that we are in — at both seen and unseen levels.

Cyndi Lane ("The Subtle Body") said even our ancestors knew about gross and subtle energy. All corners of the world had their own understanding of the energetic body, including the Hindu, Chinese, Tibetan, Mayan, Cherokee, Incan, Egyptian and African versions. They knew that the energy centers (chakras) could transform one type of energy into the other and back again.

Thus, our body is made of some parts we can see, like the *gross physical body* with skin, hair, muscles, etc. (below, left) and some parts we cannot see with our eyes, like the *subtle energetic body* with the auric layers, chakras, etc. (below, right).

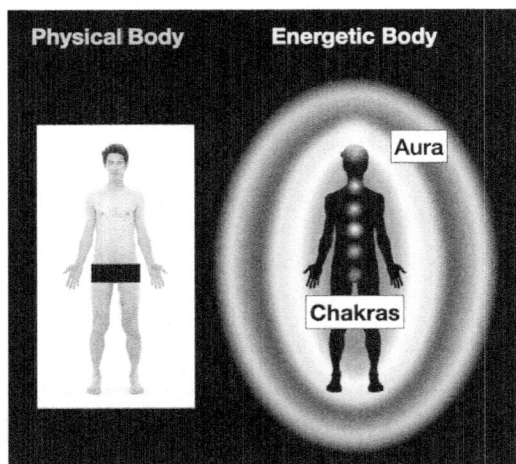

The amazing thing is that the soul's energy is very focused, like a laser beam that creates our *physical body* — a human form to have a physical experience in our "3D" reality. Every **organ** in the physical body has an *etheric counterpart* in the subtle energetic body. The physical organs (e.g. liver) can only process gross physical energy provided by the food and drink we consume. But the subtle energy organs (e.g. etheric liver) can process both gross and subtle energies. How?

How many chakras are there? There are three sizes of chakras: major, minor and mini-chakras distributed around the body wherever energy lines meet or create energy junctures. The subtle energy veins (nadi/meridians) run along the same lines as the blood vessels and nerves do.

We use seven major chakras or energy centers or to bring in *life force energy* (prana/chi) from the surrounding environment into the body. This energy is free and all around us. The chakras are energy transformers that shift energy from a higher to a lower frequency and vice versa. As Cyndi Lane ("The Subtle Body") wrote, the chakras are the power centers that run the "you inside of you" and each chakra is paired with a corresponding auric layer that regulates the "you outside of you." The aura ("biofield") serves as a layer of energetic protection.

Think of the subtle energetic body as an onion with seven layers. We could view all the layers and chakras at the same time like the cross-section of an onion (below, left) or look at just one layer at a time, such as the third chakra and its aura (below, right).

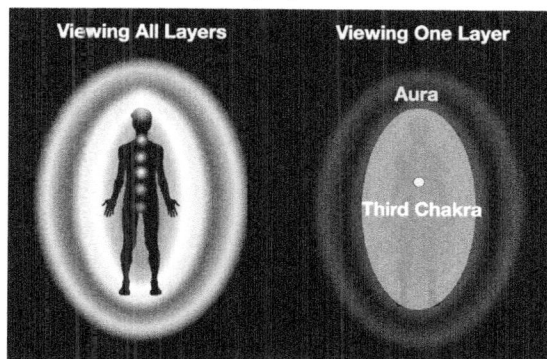

14

These major chakras are not unique to humans. All animals have them, too, because they exist at the same physical environment as us (below). The animals do us a big favor by being here. One of the ways they serve us is to clean up and realign the stagnant lower frequency energies in our physical environment that higher level maintenance entities cannot access.

Most people are completely unaware of this function — animals maintain the biosphere of the planet for us and all the other living entities that are here. They also serve as our companions and as a source of physical food until we will outgrow that as a species.

As human beings start to ascend in frequency, the bottom three chakras will consolidate into one **composite chakra** that supports the physical body at FB 1-3. At that point, we will have just five chakras (below).

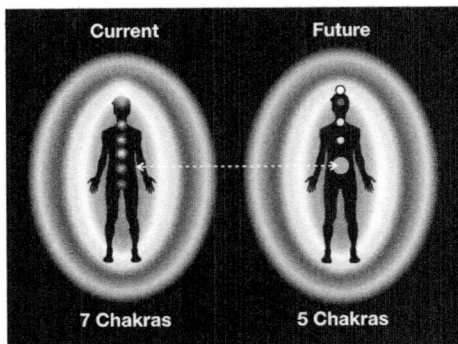

Then as we continue to ascend to FB 4 (lower astral level), we will have just four chakras (at FB 4-5-6-7), because we won't need the gross physical chakras. They become redundant. In the future, chakras 4 and 5 will also consolidate into one composite chakra that combines the heart and throat chakra functions. Then we will have just three chakras. But the upper two chakras (third eye and crown) will stay separate, because of their higher functionality.

At even higher levels (FB 8-12) in the physical universe, we won't need any chakras at all, because we will be purely *energetic entities* with more gaseous forms (see "Spiritual Guide To Our Multiverse"). The analogy is that our physical body is solid like ice at FB 1-3, our astral bodies are like water at FB 4-7 and our higher bodies are gaseous like steam at FB 8-12.

How many planes do we exist on? The human form is quite complicated. When the soul gets closer to the body, it needs to "step down" the soul's higher energies a few notches before they can enter the body without blowing a fuse, so to speak. That's why we have **three energy centers** *above* the head that funnel the energies from frequency level 10 to level 9 to level 8.

That means our human form is present on three different planes of existence (below):

• The purely energetic or gaseous form exists on the **Energetic plane** at FB 8-9-10.

• The semi-physical or light bodies exist on the **Astral plane** at FB 4-5-6-7.

• The gross physical or solid body exists on the **Physical plane** at FB 1-2-3.

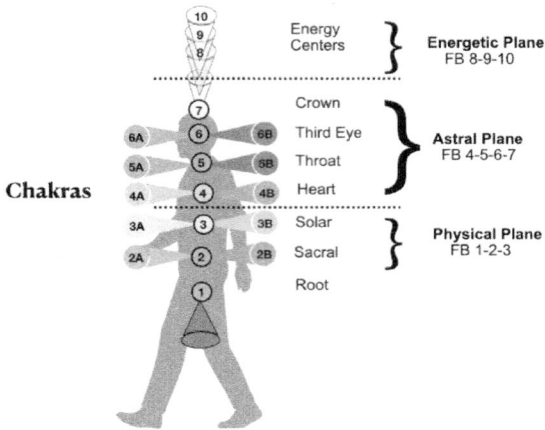

We are built like a walking vortex! That's how the energies can go down the Hara line to enter at the **seventh chakra** (at the crown or top of the head) and go down the central channel to the **sixth chakra** (third eye behind the forehead), **fifth chakra** (throat level), **fourth chakra** (heart level), **third chakra** (solar plexus halfway between the navel and sternum), **second chakra** (sacral below the navel) and **first chakra** (at the root, perineum or base of the legs).

Each major chakra works with energies at one particular **frequency band** — from FB 7 at the seventh chakra to FB 1 at the first chakra (above). Note that the crown chakra and root chakras have a single funnel (pointing up to "heaven" at FB 7 and down to "earth" at FB 1), while all the other chakras in the middle have two funnels (pointing to the front and the back of the body).

How do the front and back chakras differ? Each chakra has a **psychological function** in terms of **Intentions** (front chakras, labeled as "A") and **Actions** (back chakras, labeled as "B" below), based on Barbara Brennan's work ("The Hands of Light").

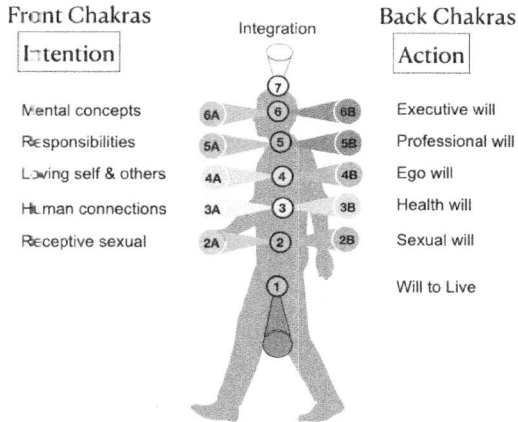

The **front chakras** are associated with our *intentions*, such as our receptive sexual function, quality of love, giving and receiving pleasure (front of the second chakra or **2A**), knowing who you are in the universe and human connectedness (**3A**), self-love and feelings of love for other humans, openness and connectedness with all life forms (**4A**), responsibility for creating what you need, taking in and assimilating knowledge (**5A**), and forming ideas, visualizing mental concepts, and conceptualizing how you see your world or reality (**6A**).

The **back chakras** are associated with our *actions*, including our will to live in a physical reality, quantity of physical energy, potency or vitality (**first chakra**), sexual will, quantity of sexual energy or potency (back of the second chakra or **2B**), health will or intention towards your physical health, also a spiritual healing center (**3B**), ego will or going for what you want, action and power, will towards the outer world (**4B**), professional will or your sense of self within your society, profession and peers (**5B**), and mental executive will or taking action to implement your ideas in a practical way to manifest them (**6B**).

18

To summarize, the front chakras are *feeling centers* (pubic 2A, solar plexus 3A, heart 4A, throat 5A), while the back chakras are *will centers* (power/energy/action) (root 1, sacral 2B, diaphragmatic 3B, between shoulder blades 4B, base of neck 5B). The head has *mental centers* (crown 7, forehead 6A, and mental executive 6B).

All these functions are *integrated* at the crown or **seventh chakra**, which represents the whole being, its sense of purpose and connection to faith and transcendence. Note that when you state an *intention* (by either visualizing it or using your mentally spoken words to state your intention), the back chakra automatically turns on as well — it's ready for *action!*

How do the chakras function? The cone-shaped chakra funnel contains a group of vortices that spin very fast to gather energies in a particular *frequency* range (below). Each vortex is made of smaller cones or minor vortices that funnel *sub-frequencies* within the same frequency band.

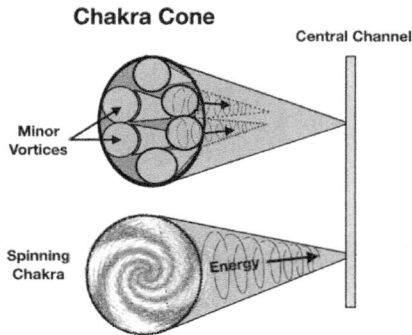

Chakra Cone

Central Channel

Minor Vortices

Spinning Chakra

Energy

Each *frequency* is not just one band. It has 12 sub-frequencies within it, and then each *sub-frequency* has 12 *sub-subfrequencies* within it for a total of 144 sub-subfrequencies at each level. That's what the minor vortices work with, pulling different sub-frequencies into our body.

When the chakras are open and fully extended as a funnel (about 30 cm away from the body) and spinning *clockwise*, they *pull in* energy from the surrounding environment toward the central Hara line in the body (above). When the chakras are spinning *counterclockwise*, they *send* energy away from the body. This is how healers send energy to others (e.g. from their heart chakra or hands to another living entity that receives that energy with their chakra, image analogy, below).

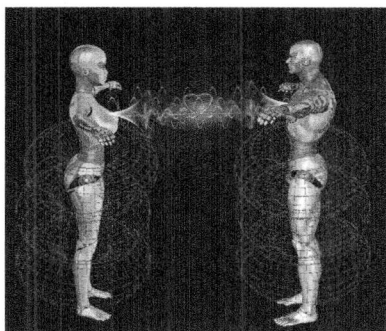

Note that the true color of the chakra energies is iridescent or colorless to the human eye, but each chakra has a characteristic *energy signature* that a healer or an experienced meditator can perceive, according to Guy Needler ("Psycho-Spiritual Healing").

The seven chakras are traditionally illustrated by rainbow colors, symbols and flower petals. For example, the first chakra is shown in red and has four petals (vortices), which can metabolize four or more sub-frequencies of energy within the first frequency band (FB 1, below).

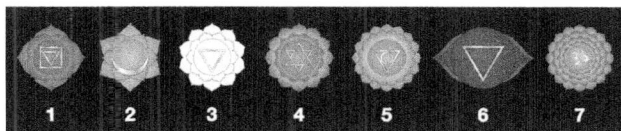

Similarly, the sacral chakra has six petals (working at FB 2) and the solar chakra has 10 petals (at FB 3). The heart chakra has 12 petals (at FB 4) and the throat chakra has 16 petals (at FB 5). The third eye chakra has 96 petals (at FB 6) and the crown chakra has 972 vortices (at FB 7), which creates the so-called "thousand-petaled lotus" described in ancient yogic texts. It is the most subtle level in the chakra system and relates to pure consciousness ("samadhi" state).

The energy from all these chakras gets *metabolized*, broken down and *blended* to create a **composite energy** that animates and nourishes the whole body. We need this blend of energy in addition to the physical food and drink we consume to exist at these low frequencies here.

At higher frequencies, we can sustain our human form using only the chakra energies (no food). By the time we ascend to the high fourth frequency level, we will use our chakras more and eat less physical food and eat less often.

What are the auric layers? In the older literature, there is some confusion or misinformation about what creates the aura or human energy field around the body. Let's clear that up with what we know today, based on Guy Needler's work ("Psycho-Spiritual Healing").

The seven chakras irradiate the **seven auric layers** (image analogy, below, left) and also feed or energize the **seven energetic templates** (below, right) that envelop the physical body layer by layer at seven levels (FB 1-7). It's a bit like wearing seven suits on top of the physical body.

The auric layers represent a *waste product* from the chakras, which are "lossy" in their function. When a chakra is working, it is taking in some energy at one frequency level, but it is also wasting some energy at that level, which accumulates around the body as an auric layer. Thus, the seven chakras create the seven auric layers as a byproduct of their wasted energy.

Auric Layers

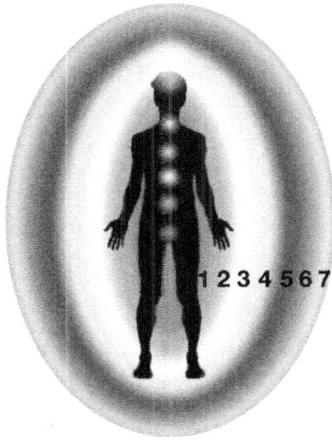

Energetic Templates

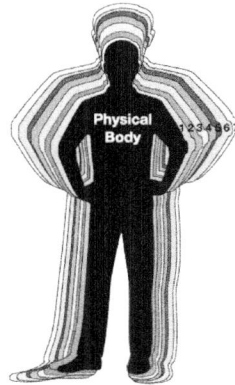

What are the energetic templates? The seven energetic templates create the physical body. The energetic templates have a 3D matrix with height, width, depth, but are "nested" or overlaid on top of each other in the same space (below). They are inflated and separated by the frequencies that are independent of each other. That's how they can exist in the same space.

Nested

Energy Templates

Seven Energetic Templates with Their Chakras

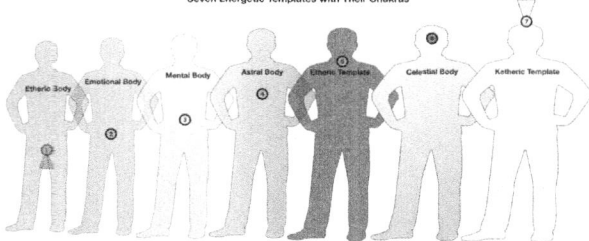

But they are linked together by the energy lines that connect the chakras, so that the templates can work together to create the physical body.

Each template is fed by one chakra at one frequency level that energizes the template at that level (above). The chakras themselves are not nested, although some older illustrations may show all seven chakras present in every template, which is not correct, according to Needler. There is only one chakra per template. But the templates are nested together, since the higher template creates the next lower one. The information is passed down the templates.

For example, the higher mental or ketheric template (at FB 7, above) creates the higher emotional or celestial body (at FB 6), which creates the higher etheric template (at FB 5), which creates the astral body (at FB 4), which creates the lower mental body (at FB 3), which creates the lower emotional body (at FB 2), which creates the etheric body (at FB 1).

Each template has a different structure and function. For example, the *ketheric template* (FB 7) has a matrix of tiny gold-silver threads of light. It contains the information about the person's life plan and past lives and holds all the auric layers together.

The *celestial body* (FB 6) is made of shimmering light with pastel colors that communicate oneness and unconditional love. The *etheric template* (FB 5) is a perfect blueprint for the etheric body at FB 1 to fill out. It looks like a photographic negative with cobalt blue fine lines.

The *astral body* (FB 4) is made of amorphous clouds of light that act as transformers of higher energy to/from physical energy (both ways). The heart chakra is where we hold *universal love* (Gate 25 of Spirit) for all entities in the universe seen as green light, and *love of humanity* (Gate 15 of Fellowship) or personal love is seen as rose/pink light. Gate 15 is common to every life form, which allows them to embrace different rhythms and behaviors in different species.

The *mental body* (FB 3) has our thought-forms and ideas seen as bright yellow light around the head and shoulders. The *emotional body* (FB 2) is made of multicolored clouds in motion that represent our emotions and feelings, which are perceived by clairvoyants as different colors (e.g. rose for unselfish love/affection, red for passion/anger, orange for ambition/pride, dark red or maroon for rage/aggression, brown for low self-esteem/egoism, black for malice-hatred, etc.). That's how they "translate" different frequencies into different colors that they perceive (below).

The etheric body (FB 1) is the blueprint for the physical body. The *etheric body* is the matrix that contains all the information from the six templates above it. The physical body is manifested as a *mirror image* of the etheric body. All the physical cells are grown and organized along the grid structure in the etheric body, which looks like a web of tiny blue energy lines (image analogy, human head viewed from various angles, below).

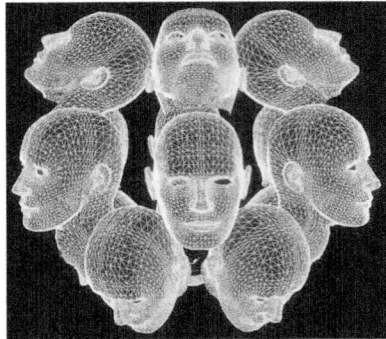

Note: The etheric body also retains the energetic blueprints for any organs or body parts removed by surgery or accident (e.g. limb amputation, gall bladder removal, hysterectomy, etc.).

How does the energetic side interface with cells? Every cell has its own aura or subtle energetic field (image analogy with simulated energetic templates and Kirlian photography, below). The field affects the permeability of substrates that need to get into the cell (e.g. water, nutrients, oxygen, etc.) or secretions that need to get out of the cell (e.g. hormones, enzymes, antibodies) and waste products that need to be removed from the cell (e.g. carbon dioxide, excess salt, water, toxins, etc.).

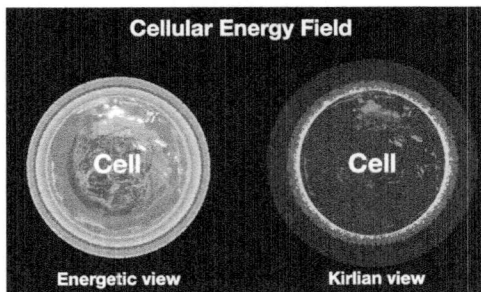

The physical vehicle can be *programmed* from the energetic templates on the "spiritual side." The physiological interface is the RNA found in every cell. That means every cell in our body is in contact with the energetic side, as described by Guy Needler ("Psycho-Spiritual Healing").

RNA is a two-way communication medium, which is first programmed by the *etheric template* and *etheric body* (image analogy, below). Then the **etheric RNA** transmits the right information to the cell's **nuclear DNA**, which passes the information through the cell's **cytoplasmic RNA** (messenger RNA for transcription of the message and transfer RNA for translation of the codons into a string of amino acids) to build the right **proteins** (shown as magenta ribbons or coils inside the cell, close up, below).

The structural and functional proteins allow the cell to differentiate into the right type of cell with the right function in the right organ or body part (e.g. liver cell, heart muscle cell, white blood cells, brain cells, nerve cells, connective tissue, etc.). By the way, there are over 30 trillion cells in the average human body that are part of this communication loop.

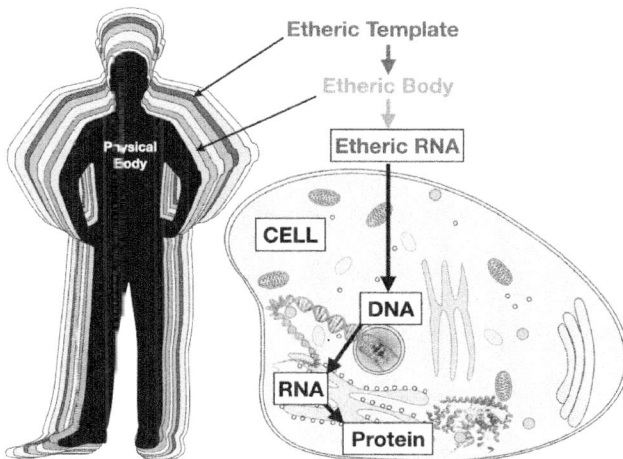

The cell's newly built protein is then checked to see if it has an acceptable form (or not). Otherwise, it is rejected by the cells in the organ, body part or the immune system. How?

There is a feedback loop from the cell back to the energetic side. The cell sends a biochemical message via the cell's RNA to the nuclear DNA, which sends an energetic response via the energetic RNA back to the original energetic template. If the original template was correctly translated on the physical side, then the template turns off any further adjustments. The person will have a feeling of well-being and ease. Otherwise, they may feel dis-ease or disease.

What's the point? I don't know about you, but to me this information is amazing. I used to be in awe and wonder of the *physical organ systems* (e.g. cardiovascular, nervous, immune, digestive, endocrine, reproductive, etc.), which are functioning in both humans and animals.

They are complex and functionally interconnected on so many levels, yet they keep us going day after day. Now that we know there is an *energetic basis* for all the functions and dysfunctions of the cells and organs, we have a better understanding of who, what, where, when, and why dis-ease occurs in our physical bodies. Let's find out more about it in the next chapter.

"All of life is Divine, and when we treat all of life as Divine, we change everything." — *Neale Donald Walsch*

CHAPTER 3

WHAT IS THE ENERGETIC BASIS OF DISEASE?

"Your physical body is a construct of your energetic field. In order to permanently change the body, you have to change the energetic programs that you are running." — *Wendy Kennedy*

What is the physical basis of disease? As a scientist, I have spent most of my life studying the physical body and the disease conditions associated with it from many different perspectives (e.g. clinical medicine and surgery, clinical pathology, anatomic pathology, molecular biology, genomic studies. testing many types of therapeutics — small molecules, recombinant proteins, antisense therapy, gene therapy, etc.). We are trying to understand, diagnose, prevent, treat or cure disease conditions with different therapies to extend the lifespan of a human or an animal.

Here is an image to illustrate the **blueprint of disease** according to western medicine. It starts with a **cell** (pink, below) with a **nucleus** (purple, below) that contains all the **chromosomes** with tightly coiled **DNA** (deoxyribonucleic acid). The DNA contains all the **gene** sequences that code for the 20,000+ structural and functional **proteins** that the cells in our physical bodies require to work properly. The rest of the genome is not "junk DNA." That's a misunderstanding.

Our genetic code has countless regulatory DNA and RNA sequences, noncoding RNA genes for dozens of different RNA types and other sequences with yet unknown functions. It's like a new language that molecular biologists are learning to speak. Just because we don't understand it doesn't make it "junk" to those who do. Scientific knowledge is always changing and evolving.

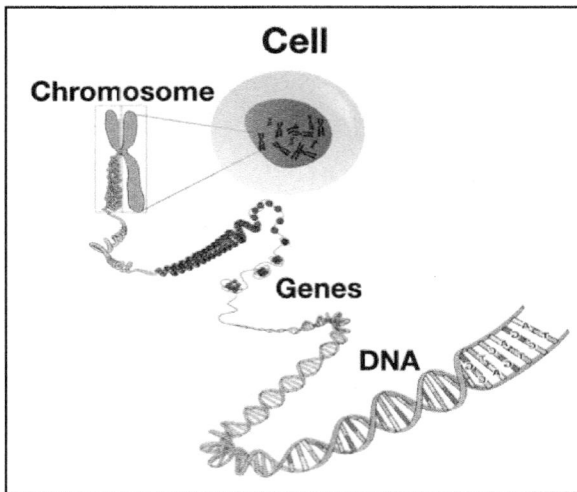

Think of **DNA** as the hardware, which is the *same* in every cell of the body, and **epigenetics** as the software, which is *different* in every cell, as observed by nutrigenomics researcher Lucia Aronica, PhD. The epigenetic phenomena occur "above the genes" to regulate the DNA. There are many **epigenetic mechanisms**, such as diet, exercise, stress, aging, emotional states, environmental exposure to toxic chemicals, ionizing radiation, etc. — all these things affect which genes are turned on or off. That affects how the cell develops into a specific cell type (e.g. brain cell vs. liver cell), and how efficiently the cell will function within an organ to produce enzymes, neurotransmitters, antibodies, collagen, muscle fibers, etc.

Sometimes genes or cells become *dysfunctional*, which may lead to conditions like cancer, infectious diseases, autoimmune diseases, diabetes, obesity, dementia, etc. The western medical approach only considers the physical side of the human body. Most people are clueless about the role of subtle energy bodies in health and disease. It's high time to change that!

Can mutant cells or genes be healed? According Guy Needler ("Psycho-Spiritual Healing") this can be done by **reprogramming** things in a particular order. First, the *DNA* needs to be reprogrammed (by removing or splicing the defect in the DNA strand energetically). Then the *energetic templates* need to be reprogrammed and followed by *psycho-spiritual reprogramming*, because the psycho-spiritual programming controls the energetic templates.

Mutant cancer cells can also be reprogrammed, but the process needs to include all seven energetic templates starting from the top down (from the ketheric template down to the etheric body). All layers need to have the right information, *and* the mutant cells need to be told to undergo programmed cell death (or apoptosis). When all seven layers are healed and modified in this way, the gross physical form will heal — provided that it is part of the person's *life plan*. In some cases, the disease condition is experienced for a while and then the person is healed. In other cases, it is part of their "**exit plan**" or the way the soul has planned to leave that lifetime (e.g. terminal cancer), so they won't heal or go into remission (Chapter 15).

What is the energetic basis of disease? Now we know that the gross physical body is a mirror image of the lower **etheric body**, which contains the energy matrix or template created from all the information from the six energetic templates above it (below).

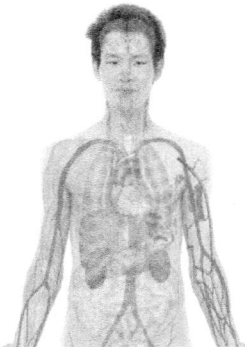

Physical Body   **Energetic Templates**

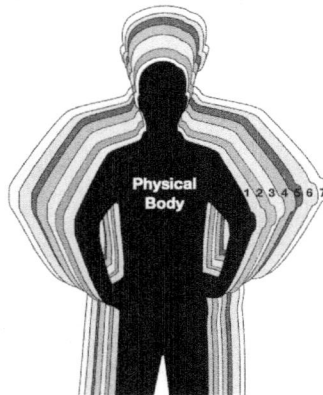

The physical body is surrounded by the lower etheric body (at FB 1), lower emotional body (FB 2), lower mental body (FB 3), astral body (FB 4), higher etheric template (FB 5), higher emotional or celestial body (FB 6), and higher mental or ketheric body (FB 7).

The physical body manifests on the level of instincts, reflexes and *automatic* functions of organs. But all the other expressions of *consciousness* come from our energetic templates. Each layer functions at its own level, but all layers are interconnected in the same space as our reality.

Illness or physical dysfunction is caused by imbalances or disharmonies in the human energy field or any of the energetic templates that change our *psycho-spiritual programming.*

When we wish to heal a physical issue (e.g. backache), we may need to repair one or more of the chakras, auric fields and seven energetic layers that may be contributing to the physical pain or illness. That means looking at what sensations, feelings, thought processes, and energetic experiences we may notice when we are in pain. The pain is just a clue to look further within to find the root of the problem.

What are the chakras associated with? The chakras don't work alone. Each major chakra is associated with a different energetic template, endocrine gland, major nerve plexus, vertebrae and energetic fields of various organs and tissues nourished by a particular chakra (below).

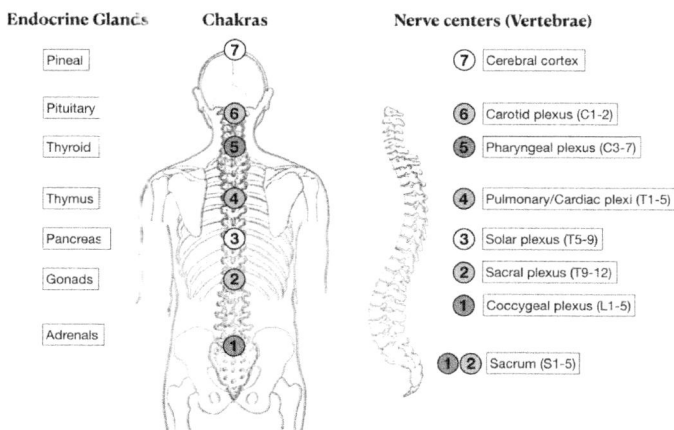

Modified from:
http://commons.wikimedia.org/wiki/File:Backbone_%28PSF%29.png?uselang=de

We also can view the chakras by Human Design (below), which is based on the I Ching and other esoteric systems, as described by Ra Uru Hu ("The Complete Rave I'Ching"). It gives us a new way to understand the **"energetic blueprint"** of a person, where each chakra has a specific set of functions ("gates") connected by specific energy circuits ("channels") within the body.

The body graph shows nine chakras, because the third and fourth chakras are split in Human Design. But in my understanding, the splits simply represent the front (A) and back (B) functions of the third and fourth chakras, labeled as 3A/solar, 3B/splenic, 4A/identity and 4B/ego (below).

Chakras By Human Design

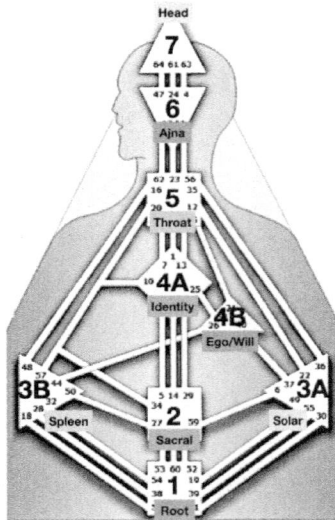

How do the gates relate to our genetic code? The I Ching system describes *duality* in terms of a *binary code* made of solid (yang) or broken (yin) lines. There are 64 "hexagrams" or "gates" in total that describe different states of "beingness." Each gate is made of six lines

stacked on top of each other in different combinations —
just like the binary code of 0s (yin) and 1s (yang).

For example, **Gate 1 of Purpose** is made of six solid
yang lines (shown as six white squares in the circle at 12
o'clock, below). Its polar opposite is **Gate 2 of Direction**,
which is the most yin gate with six broken lines (shown as
six black squares at 6 o'clock, below). Amazingly, these
lines also correspond to our **genetic code** (below, middle).
How so?

I Ching	Genetic Code	Human Design

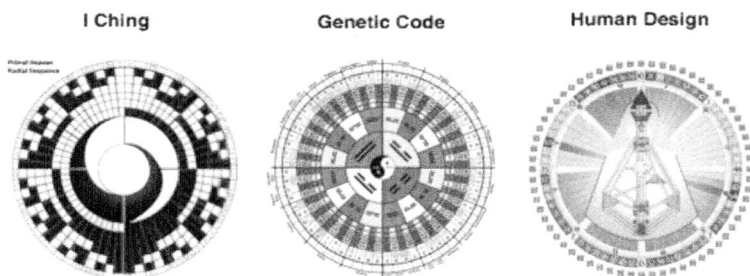

Our DNA has specific codons or nucleotide triplets
(made of Adenine, Guanine, Cytosine, and Thymine in
DNA or Uracil in RNA) that encode **20 different amino
acids**. They are the building blocks of life used to make
proteins that make up about 20% of our body composition.

**Each amino acid is encoded by one to six different
codons** that correspond to one to six specific I Ching Gates
(below). For example, in the Figure below, **Codon 1** is the
triplet called **AUG** (made of Adenine, Uracil and Guanine)
in the messenger RNA (mRNA) sequence, which codes for
the amino acid called **Methionine** that corresponds to **Gate
41** represented by a unique binary code hexagram (below).
There is only one codon that corresponds to Methionine.

Binary Code

	Codon 1	Codon 2	Codon 3	Codon 4	
Genetic Code	AUG	ACC	CAA	CUU	··· mRNA
Amino Acid	Methionine	Threonine	Glutamine	Leucine	··· Protein
I Ching Gate	41	5	13	24	
Hexagram					

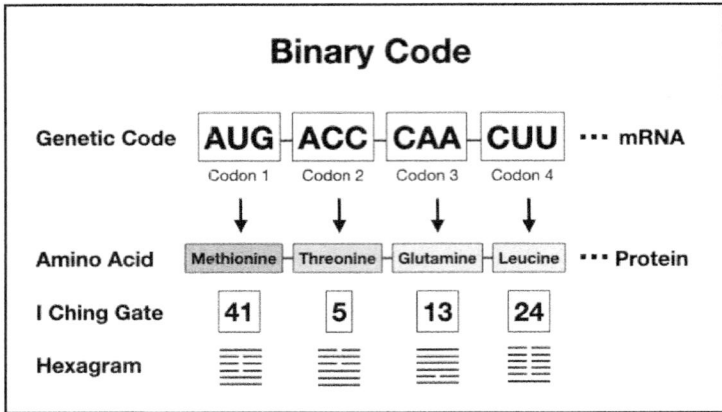

Similarly, **Codon 4** (codon CUU) encodes for the amino acid **Leucine** represented by **Gate 24** (above). But Leucine can also be encoded by five other codons: **Gate 3** (CUC), **Gate 27** (CUG), **Gate 42** (CUA), **Gate 20** (UUA) and **Gate 23** (UUG). They create a "family of codons."

Amino Acid Functions

BRAIN
Tyrosine - 31, 62
Phenylalanine - 2, 8
Tryptophan - 35
Glutamine - 13, 30
Glutamate - 44, 50
Aspartate - 28, 32
Histidine - 49, 55
Glycine - 6, 40, 47, 64
Arginine - 10, 17, 21, 25, 38, 51
Serine - 15, 39, 52, 53, 54, 58

LIVER
Methionine - 41
Threonine - 5, 9, 11, 26
Glutamine - 49, 55
Cysteine - 16, 45
Glycine - 6, 40, 47, 64
Arginine - 10, 17, 21, 25, 38, 51

MUSCLE
Valine - 4, 7, 29, 59
Isoleucine - 19, 60, 61
Leucine - 3, 20, 23, 24, 27, 42
Glutamine - 13, 30
Lysine - 1, 14
Cysteine - 16, 45
Glycine - 6, 40, 47, 64
Alanine - 18, 46, 48, 57
Arginine - 10, 17, 21, 25, 38, 51

BONES & FASCIA
Histidine - 49, 55
Lysine - 1, 14
Proline - 22, 36, 37, 63
Glycine - 6, 40, 47, 64

PITUITARY & PINEAL GLAND
Aspartate - 28, 32
Glycine - 6, 40, 47, 64
Arginine - 10, 17, 21, 25, 38, 51

SKIN
Cysteine - 16, 45
Lysine - 1, 14
Proline - 22, 36, 37, 63
Threonine - 5, 9, 11, 26

IMMUNITY
Lysine - 1, 14
Histidine - 49, 55
Isoleucine - 19, 60, 61
Alanine - 18, 46, 48, 57

HYPOTHALAMUS
Phenylalanine - 2, 8

THYROID
Tyrosine - 31, 62
Phenylalanine - 2, 8

LUNGS
Cysteine - 16, 45
Arginine - 10, 17, 21, 25, 38, 51

HEART
Lysine - 1, 14
Methionine - 41
Arginine - 10, 17, 21, 25, 38, 51

BLOOD
Cysteine - 16, 45
Histidine - 49, 55
Tryptophan - 35
Serine - 15, 39, 52, 53, 54, 58

GASTROINTESTINAL TRACT
Glutamine - 13, 30
Glutamate - 44, 50
Histidine - 49, 55
Alanine - 18, 46, 48, 57
Glycine - 6, 40, 47, 64
Serine - 15, 39, 52, 53, 54, 58

PANCREAS
Cysteine - 16, 45
Glutamate - 13, 30

KIDNEYS & ADRENALS
Glutamine - 13, 30
Arginine - 10, 17, 21, 25, 38, 51

Note: The amino acid name is followed by one or more Gates that correspond to it

All the amino acids have specific functions in different organs and tissues around the body (below). The **amino acid pool** is used to make peptides and proteins for many different functions, such as building body proteins, enzymes, hormones, cell signaling, reproduction, appetite, behavior, metabolic regulation, growth and development, body composition, energy substrates, blood flow, fluid balance, acid/base balance, RNA and DNA synthesis, immunity, tissue repair, etc.

How do the gates relate to chakras and organs? Using Human Design to construct the energetic blueprint of the body, we can map the **64 Gates** to seven major **chakras** (below) that are assigned to represent particular organs and tissues, based on the work of Ra Uru Hu ("The Complete Rave I'Ching") and Richard Rudd ("Gene Keys").

64 Gates of the Body

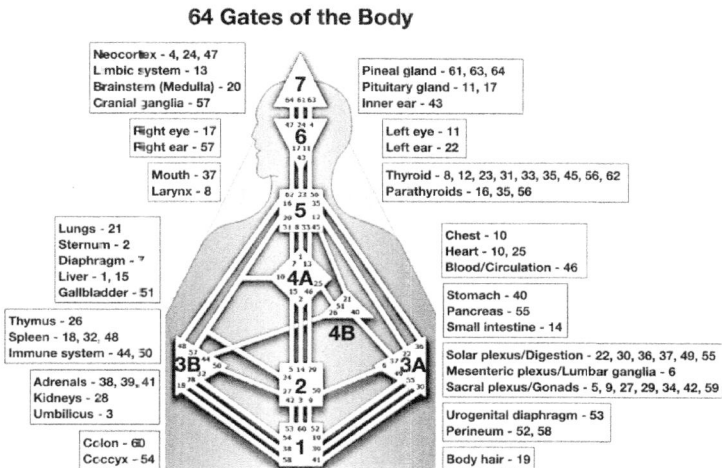

As a scientist, when I look at these gate/organ associations, it seems like an oversimplification of the billions of physiologic functions carried out by the physical body. But it's not meant to be taken literally. Think of each gate as a "tuning dial" that can be turned up or down to attune to a certain frequency range associated with a particular chakra function.

For example, **Gate 57** is called The Gentle/Penetrating Wind in the I Ching system. In Human Design, it maps to the right ear. Gate 57 is also called the **Gate of Intuition and Clairaudience**, which is about having acoustic or vibrational sensitivity (e.g. hearing high pitched sounds, which can sound like tinnitus or Morse code).

If the person only hears tinnitus, it may be due to their refusal to listen or not hearing the inner voice or lack of self-trust. When the person learns to "translate" the auditory signal into a higher intuitive function, they will hear the inner truth and have natural psychic abilities, intuitive insight and clarity. That's the true function of Gate 57. These types of gate associations with higher energetic functions go above and beyond the purely physical functions of the organs.

We may perceive the information in terms of images (called clairvoyance), sounds (clairaudience), feeling or sensing changes in the physical body (clairsentience), instant knowingness (clair-cognizance), intuitive dreaming, or other "clairs."

Here is a list of higher intuitive functions, based on Karen Curry's work ("Understanding Human Design"). Different functions are associated with different gates and/ or energy channels that connect different chakras to work together (below). **These are our "superpowers!"**

We all have some of these higher functions built-in to our energetic blueprint. For example, **superconsciousness** (above) means "channeling" or having connectivity to

Higher Intuitive Functions

Clairaudience = Hearing	Claircognizance = Knowing	Clairsentience = Feeling Self	Superconsciousness or "Angelic" channeling

• Gate 57 (right ear)***
 • Gate 22 (left ear)
 • Gate 43 (inner ear)
 • Channel 22-12 (openness, "voice channel")
 • Integration circuit
     • Channel 34-57***
     • Channel 20-57
     • Channel 10-57
 • Centering circuit
     • Channel 25-51
     • Channel 10-34
 • Knowing circuit
     • Channel 61-24
     • Channel 23-43
     • Channel 1-8
     • Channel 2-14
     • Channel 12-22
     • Channel 20-57
     • Channel 3-60
     • Channel 28-38
     • Channel 39-55
	• Gate 57 (most intuitive)
	 • Knowing circuit
	     • Channel 61-24
	     • Channel 23-43
	     • Channel 1-8
	     • Channel 2-14
	     • Channel 12-22
	     • Channel 20-57
	     • Channel 3-60
	     • Channel 28-38
	     • Channel 39-55
		• Any Open Centers
		 • Sensing circuit
		     • Channel 64-47
		     • Channel 11-56
		     • Channel 13-33
		     • Channel 29-46
		     • Channel 42-53
		     • Channel 35-36
		     • Channel 30-41
		 • Sensitivity/attunement to animals, nature spirits
		     • Channel 19-49
		     • Gate 19*** or 49***
		 • Sensitivity to all life forms in nature (plants, animals)
		     • Gate 15*** (love of humanity and nature)
		     • Gate 5 (flow)
		     • Channel 5-15 (cycles, rhythms)
			• Channel 63-4
			 • Channel 61-24
			 • Channel 64-47
			 • Channel 11-56
			 • Channel 23-43
			 • Channel 16-48
			 • Channel 13-33
			 • Channel 7-31
			 • Channel 5-15
			 • Channel 2-14
			 • Channel 29-46
			 • Channel 10-34
			 • Channel 50-27
			 • Channel 9-52
			 • Channel 3-60
			 • Channel 18-58
			 • Gate 17
			 • Gate 59
			 • Gate 54

Pure Instinct - Chakra 3B
 	
 • Gate 57 (know future)
 • Gate 48 (know enough)
 • Gate 44 (know past)
 • Gate 50 (feel values)
 • Gate 32 (see timing)
 • Gate 28 (know worth)
 • Gate 18 (know remedy)
 • Medical intuitive - open splenic chakra (3B)
	Clairvoyance = Sight
	
	 • Gate 61 (pineal)
	 • Gate 63 (pineal)
	 • Gate 64 (pineal)
	 • Defined chakra 7
	 • Logical circuit for understanding sight
	     • Channel 63-4
	     • Channel 17-62
	     • Channel 16-48
	     • Channel 7-31
	     • Channel 5-15
	     • Channel 9-52
	     • Channel 18-58
	
	 Clairgustance = Taste
	 • Gate 48 (intuitive taste)
	
	 Clairtaction = Touch
	 • Gate 19*** (attunement and supersensitivity)
		Empathy = Feeling Others with Any Open Centers or Chakras
		 • 7 read others' inspirations
		 • 6 read others' minds
		 • 5 speak for others
		 • 4A read others' identities
		 • 4B read others' willpower
		 • 3A true empath of feelings
		 • 3B medical intuitive
		 • 2 feel others' life force
		 • 1 feel others' pressure or adrenaline energy
			Intuitive Dreaming
			 • Gate 61 (inner truth)
			 • Gate 64 (abstraction)
			 • Gate 63 (logic)
			
			 Clairolfactance = Smell
			 • Gate 44 (intuitive smell)
			 • Gate 26 ("BS meter")
			 • Channel 44-26

NOTE: Gates or Channels shown with asterisks (***) have extra functionality

higher wisdom from "angelics" (meaning your guide, helpers or other nonphysical entities), Higher Self and/or Source (see "Spiritual Guide To Our Awakening").

Similary, **claircognizance** ("clear knowing") is associated with the "knowing circuit" that connects the seventh to sixth chakra (via the channel of Gates 61-24), sixth to fifth chakra (via Gates 43-23), fifth to fourth chakra (via Gates 1-8), fifth to third chakra 3A (via Gates 12-22), fifth to third chakra 3B (via Gates 20-57), fourth to second chakra (via Gates 2-14), and second to first chakra (via Gates 60-3). Nobody has all of these gates and channels in their blueprint.

But if you have one or more of these gates or channels in your blueprint, claircognizance (or knowingness) may be one of the potential "superpowers" that you are either born with (if you come in as a higher frequency individual) or can develop over time (if you are able to raise your frequency level by working on yourself and honing that function with practice).

The same goes for all the other higher functions that are built-in to our amazing human form that can sense not just with five physical senses, but dozens of extrasensory or higher intuitive functions. All we need to do is learn to use them!

Our souls "wrote" them in to our **unique soul blueprint** before we came here. In essence, each gate is associated with a unique function or state of consciousness, which may be associated with different thoughts, emotions, sensations, and/or actions that are designed to help us navigate this level of existence on the Earth.

This blueprint is part of your life plan, which sets up the potential to develop certain *soul gifts* (e.g. skills and talents brought to this life) and certain *soul challenges* (e.g. opportunity to release some physical, emotional, mental or spiritual patterns from other lives).

What's in your life plan? One way to find out is to get a Life Plan Reading from me at my website: BigPictureQuestions(dot)com (see Services tab).

How does all this translate to disease? When we look at the **physical body**, we can map the 64 Gates to different *chakras*, organs and tissues whose function is regulated by them. When we look at **physical disorders** in various organs or tissues, we can map them to specific *body fields* supplied by the chakras that energize them. Here are some examples of specific disorders associated with specific chakras in energy medicine (below).

Chakra	Body Field	Disorders
7		Brain tumor, Dementia, Coma, Amnesia, Delusions, Migraines
6		Headaches, Glaucoma, Vision, Ear, Nose Problems
5		Lung disease, Asthma, Neck, Throat, Thyroid, Parathyroids
4		Heart disease, Hypertension, Circulation, Arms, Hands, Fingers Immune deficiency (thymus)
3		Diabetes, Gallstones, Hepatitis, Fatty liver, Stomach ulcer, Irritable bowel syndrome, Eating disorders
2		Ovarian or Prostate cancer, Sexual dysfunction, Obesity, Spleen, Bladder, Low back pain
1		Arthritis, Kidney disease, Hips, Knees, Ankles, Feet, Adrenal Exhaustion, Eating disorders

For example, diabetes and hypoglycemia are disorders of the endocrine pancreas, which is energized by the third chakra (solar plexus), which is involved with various digestive disorders.

Note: This data is based on many sources, including Anodea Judith ("Eastern Body, Western Mind"), Guy Needler ("Psycho-Spiritual Healing"), Barbara Brennan ("Hands of Light"), Richard Barrett ("A New Psychology of Human Well-Being"), Richard Rudd ("Gene Keys"), Lynda Bunnell & Ra Uru Hu ("The Definitive Book of Human Design"), Karen Curry ("Understanding Human Design"), Chetan Parkyn ("The Book of Lines") and others.

What is chakra imbalance? It is said that our body is like an instrument through which our consciousness plays its music. At times, we may go out of tune. Why?

We may have some *unbalanced chakras* that influence the way we relate to the world. This Table summarizes the major chakra functions and dysfunctions that reflect either a *deficiency* (underexpression) or an *excess* (over-expression) of energy flow through particular chakras.

Chakra	Function	Endocrine Gland & Body Field	Examples of Deficiency	Examples of Excess
1 Root	Physical health, vitality, comfort, safety, security, prosperity	Adrenals: kidneys, skeleton, spinal column, bones, legs, large intestine	· Fearful, anxious, restless · Underweight, poor finances · Poor boundaries or focus · Poor discipline, disorganized	· Sluggish, tired, low energy · Greed, hoarding, obesity · Rigid boundaries, limits · Want security, fear change
2 Sacral	Sexuality, desire, needs, pleasure, touching, feeling, emotions (EQ)	Ovaries/Testes: sexual organs, uterus, prostate, spleen, urinary bladder	· Lack desire & passion · Fear sexuality & sensuality · Rigid body & attitudes · Poor social skills, numb	· Emotional dependency · Sexual addiction, seduction · Crisis junkie, mood swings · Obsessive attachment
3 Solar Plexus	Energy, activity, will, self-esteem, power, autonomy, individuation	Pancreas: stomach, gallbladder, liver, small intestine, gut nervous system	· Low self-esteem, weak will · Victim mentality, blaming · Easily manipulated, passive · Cold physically, emotionally	· Dominating, competitive · Power hungry, controlling · Arrogant, hyperactive · Manipulative, stubborn
4 Heart	Love, relationship, self-love, balance, compassion, empathy	Thymus: heart, blood, vagus nerve, arms, hands, circulation, breasts	· Depression, antisocial, cold · Intolerant, judgmental · Narcissism, lack empathy · Loneliness, fear intimacy	· Codependent, clingy · Overly sacrificing, jealous · Poor boundaries, needy · Demanding in relationships
5 Throat	Communication, listening, finding own voice, creativity	Thyroid/Parathyroids: throat, larynx, pharynx, mouth, neck, lungs, esophagus	· Fear speaking, persecution · Introvert, shy, weak voice · Poor rhythm, tone deaf · Can't articulate feelings	· Dominating, loud voice · Interrupts others, gossiping · Poor listener, deaf to others · Poor comprehension
6 Third Eye	Dreams, visions, insights, intuition, imagination, visualization	Pituitary: lower brain, ears, nose, teeth, sinuses, left eye, autonomic NS	· Denial of reality, opinionated · Poor dream recall/memory · Poor vision, insensitivity · Only one true and right way	· Delusions, hallucinations · Difficulty concentrating · Nightmares, obsessions · Oversensitive to stimuli
7 Crown	Understanding, belief systems, knowing, wisdom, transcendence	Pineal: cerebral cortex, central nervous system, skull, right eye	· Rigid belief systems · Spiritual cynic or skeptic · Learning difficulties · Apathy, doubt	· Confused, overintellectual · Disassociated from body · Disembodied mind · Spiritual addiction to guru

Over a person's lifetime, the chakras also undergo wear and tear and may become mildly disfigured or severely distorted, atrophied, inflamed or clogged with stagnated energy, astral entities or energetic foreign bodies, which affect the chakra's ability to receive life force energy and energize the templates. At some point, this will result in physical dysfunction and disease.

That's why our chakras may need some repair or reconstruction, as noticed by experienced energy healers like Guy Needler ("Psycho-Spiritual Healing") and others.

What is the origin of disease? Louise Hay ("You Can Heal Your Life") was one of the early pioneers who made the connection between negative thought patterns and various physical conditions. She discovered two basic mental patterns that contribute to disease:

Fear (e.g. tension, anxiety, nervousness, worry, doubt, insecurity, feeling not good enough or unworthy) or **anger** (e.g. resentment, frustration, impatience, irritation, criticism, jealousy or bitterness). She made a list of conditions (e.g. AIDS, addictions, cancer, arthritis, etc.) with probable emotional and mental causes and offered new thought patterns and affirmations to heal the conditions. She had miraculously healed herself of cancer in this way.

Some people (especially medical doctors) may balk at this "metaphysical way" of looking at diseases as being too simplistic given the multifactorial causes of disease. But it's no coincidence that the same *fear* and *anger* patterns are seen as the **shadow** expressions of the 64 Gates as well.

Every gate can be *underexpressed* in **fear** (where the ego shuts down) or *overexpressed* in **anger** (where the ego lashes out). Every gate can also be expressed at **higher frequencies**, which describe the **64 gifts** and **siddhis** that we aspire to develop in life, such as joy, bliss, peace, purity, harmony, awakening, ascension, etc. (see "Spiritual Guide To Our Relationships").

When we put this information together with the **seven energetic templates** that transmit information about any imbalances or disharmonies from the top down to the physical body, we can see the connection of the **psycho-spiritual programming** happening in all these layers that include both lower and higher etheric, emotional and mental functions (Chapter 2).

Guy Needler ("Psycho-Spiritual Healing") said the **origin of the physical or psycho-spiritual issues** may be related to certain feelings, emotions, past memories, frustrations, physical pain, fears, likes/dislikes, foods, accidents, past or recent experiences, psychological issues and/or energetic links with other people (e.g. family, friends, coworkers, etc.). That's why we may need *psycho-spiritual reprogramming* to resolve our issues, but there are clues found in our bodies and personalities.

How do our bodies reflect the flow of energy? Psychotherapist Wilhelm Reich ("Character Analysis") discovered a long time ago that people with similar childhood experiences and child/parent relationships had similar **bodies** and **psychological traits**.

How is that possible? Most people fit into five basic **"character structures,"** which become *coping strategies* anchored in the body (below).

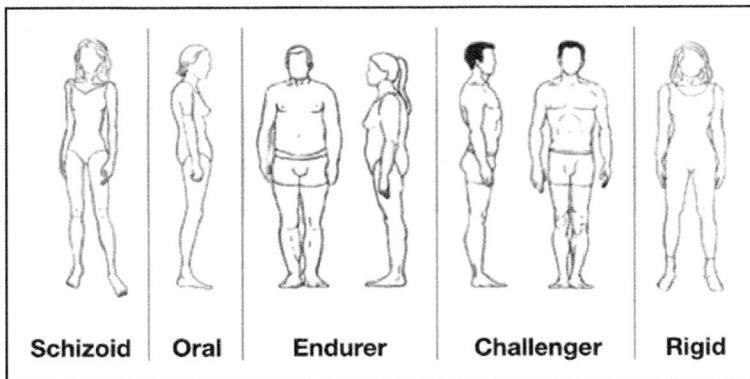

| Schizoid | Oral | Endurer | Challenger | Rigid |

These character structures reflect how the flow of energy through the body creates different types of mental, emotional and behavioral patterns. They become our unconscious defensive strategies ("body armor") that are summarized in the next Table (below, based on various sources).

Character Structure	SCHIZOID Ungrounded Fragmented	ORAL Needy Merging	ENDURER Masochist Compressed	CHALLENGER Defender Controlling	RIGID Achiever or Hysteric
Strengths	Creative mind, intelligent	Very loving, compassionate	Steady, patient, diplomatic	Leader, kind to underdogs	High achiever, successful
Illusion	My mind is my body	Love will solve everything	I'm trying to please you	It's all a matter of will	Performance is everything
Personality symptoms	Fear, anxiety, lacks sense of self, detached	Fatigue, needy, dependent, depressed	Tension, feels stuck, moody, boiling inside	Power hungry, obstinate, rage, confrontational	Competitive, proud but feel inadequate
Fear of...	Falling apart, going crazy	Abandonment, rejection	Humiliation, exposure	Submission to another being	Surrendering to feelings
because	It's not safe to be here or in my body (fear)	I'm not enough, there's not enough for me (greed)	It's not safe to follow my urges for pleasure (shame)	I can't trust others, I feel betrayed (trust, control)	It's not safe to give my love, I fear intimacy (approval)
Parents (trauma)	Fearful, angry, unwilling mom, neglect	Depriving of touch, attention, affection	Overly controlling, intrusive, shaming	Authoritarian + other seductive manipulator	Cold, rejecting father, betrayal at heart level
Wounded child	Unwanted child	Undernourished child	Overmanaged child	Betrayed child	Hurried child
Demands his/her right	To be here, to exist	To be nurtured, to have needs	To act, to be independent, autonomous	To be free, to be supported, encouraged	To want, to have feelings (love/sex)
Energy levels	Hyperactive Ungrounded (up and out)	Hypoactive Low energy (hold on)	Hypoactive Internalized (hold in)	Hyperactive then collapsed (hold up)	Hyperactive High energy (hold back)
Chakras most affected	Deficient 1st	Excessive 2nd and 4th	Blocked 3rd	Excessive 3rd, strong 5th	Deficient 4th
Healing and maturation by	Embodiment, connection, stronger boundaries	Inner love, own your needs, stand on your own two feet	Inner power, self-assertion, be free, open to spirituality	Inner wealth, learning basic trust, show vulnerability	Inner peace, open heart, connect heart to genitals

Note that each character structure is associated with *dysfunctions* in particular **chakras**. We may identify with aspects of more than one type, because we develop different coping strategies to deal with each parent (e.g. rigid pattern with father, endurer pattern with mother). Sometimes they become activated by major life stresses (e.g. death of a loved one, accident, pandemic, job loss, divorce, moving, life-threatening or severe illness, etc.). That is part of the soul's life plan.

"Love who and what you are and what you do. Laugh at yourself and at life, and nothing can touch you. It's all temporary anyway." — Louise Hay *("You Can Heal Your Life")*

What's the point? It is to show that there is a lot more to our physical health and well-being than just the physical aspect of the body. There are epigenetic, environmental, psychological, energetic, ancestral, past life and spiritual aspects that also influence our state of being.

Guy Needler's book "Psycho-Spiritual Healing" describes how an experienced energy healer works with various techniques to treat many illnesses, physical diseases and mental dysfunctions.

Anodea Judith's book "Eastern Body, Western Mind" blends psychology and spirituality into an eye-opening journey of self-exploration and self-healing. In its pages you will find yourself, your parents, siblings, partner, children and everybody else who may be dysfunctional but significant in your life. By the end, you can't help but see them in a new light with much more forgiveness and compassion for all, including yourself.

If you think you are beyond these "issues" — think again! We all have our "moments" — that's what being human is all about on this "planet of emotion." Remember you are the experiencer, but the experience is not who you are. Big difference!

We are healing unresolved *intergenerational* trauma, not just our own trauma, which takes some effort, time and courage. This is a huge task in terms of human evolution as a species. It's not a job for wimps! That's why YOU are here — thank you for your service to humanity.

"Do unto others as you would have it done to you, because it IS being done unto you! That is the Golden Rule. And now you understand it completely." — *Neale Donald Walsch* .

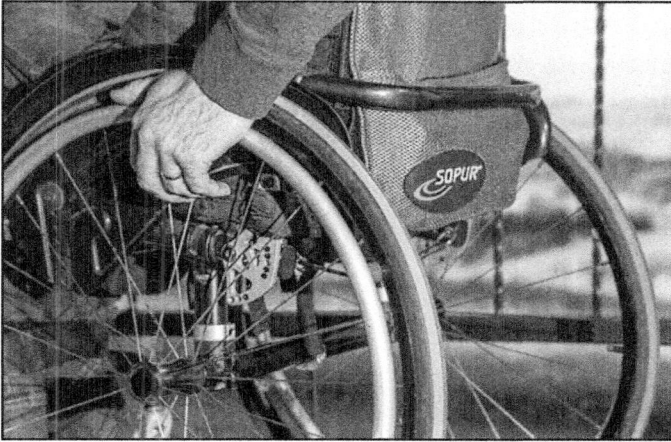

CHAPTER 4

WHAT IS THE BASIS OF PHYSICAL OR MENTAL DISABILITY?

Now that we know more about how dis-ease or disease arises, let's take a look at some specific conditions, including mental and physical disabilities, which are often misunderstood.

How do different cultures deal with disabled people? Over the centuries, our attitudes and perceptions towards people with disabilities have varied from one culture to another. Sometimes children that were visibly deformed (e.g. a six-fingered baby) or mentally retarded were killed at birth or abandoned in the wild, neglected, underfed or banished from the tribe, according to Deborah Kaplan (Independent Living Articles). They were considered inferior, unfit, shameful, cursed or possessed by evil spirits that had to be exorcised or prayed away in painful rituals.

By the Renaissance, people that were blind, deaf, mentally retarded or physically disabled were sent to asylums or institutions for life and marginalized from society. Then in the early 20th century, the eugenics movement led to medical experimentation, sterilization and euthanasia of what they considered to be "defective" people, followed by mass extermination of Jews, gypsies, gays, lesbians and other "deviants" during World War II.

Franklin Roosevelt was the first disabled U.S. president, but he tried to hide his paraplegia from the public. After the war, the return of disabled veterans led to rehabilitation, education and vocational training programs. People with disabilities did not receive legal protection from discrimination until 1990 in the U.S., but nowadays they're integrated into homes, schools and work-places. We've come a long way, but they still face many forms of discrimination.

How do we define disability? Deborah Kaplan noted that "disability" is really a social construct that covers a whole spectrum of conditions with many questions. What makes one condition a visible disability and another a socially acceptable impairment (e.g. eyeglasses, walker, hearing aids, below)?

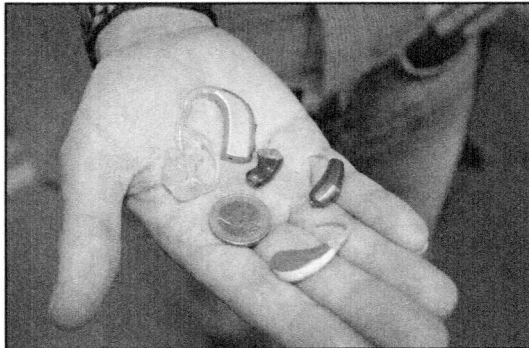

What about invisible conditions, such as cochlear implants, a prosthetic limb, or genetic markers for a disease? What about disabled people who lead independent lives, like partially paralyzed artist AleXsandro Palombo, who wants to promote awareness of "ableism?"

"How wonderful would it be if Snow White was a wheelchair user who still managed to care for the seven dwarves and her personality made the prince marry her not her appearance." —AleXsandro Palombo

This line will be even more blurred by the newer devices that will enhance the function of body parts (e.g. artificial limbs, retina, etc.) and prolong our lifespan in the future.

Is disability fate or a random event? Before we incarnate in human form, our souls set up a **life plan** and decide what we wish to experience. We make several contracts with other souls who agree to play certain roles in our life, such as a parent, sibling, mate, etc. (see "Spiritual Guide To Our Relationships").

For example, your soul might choose to experience a physical disability, such as blindness and decide if the condition will be congenital (present at birth) or acquired later in life. If we are born blind, we don't know what it's like to have vision, so we don't miss it. We may develop our other senses (e.g. hearing, touch, intuition or "sixth sense") to a more heightened level.

If we are born with vision, but develop blindness later — in early childhood, midlife or old age — the contrast between having vs. not having that visual sensory input is dramatic. We might learn to adapt by developing hyperacuity in other senses, such as hearing (below). In any case, it creates a very different experience from having sight.

What is the purpose of disability? In some cases, the soul chooses a physical or mental disability to limit the scope of life, to have fewer choices, so they can focus on one or two major issues fully, as reported by José Stevens, PhD ("The Michael Handbook") and others.

It allows them to reduce distractions, so they're induced to be more introspective or to contemplate and re-evaluate experiences in this and other lifetimes. It may be a so-called "resting lifetime" between busy, challenging or growth-oriented lifetimes, or one where the person wants to experience childlike simplicity, innocence or feel oneness with creation, to be in awe and wonder with the beauty of a flower or a cloud in the sky, as noted by Aaron Christeaan et al. ("Michael: The Basic Teachings").

In other cases, the purpose is to find inner strength to overcome the "dysfunctional mold" they are put in, to show that physical form does not have to be restrictive. That's what Helen Keller said to Peter Jenkins and Toni Ann Winninger ("Talking with Twentieth-Century Women"), who interviewed her soul on the Other Side.

Helen was born healthy, but contracted scarlet fever before age 2, which left her deaf and blind. She found things by brushing them with her hands and feet, and sensed other things energetically by feeling the vibration (like sonar) sent off by them (e.g. wall). By age 7, she had developed her own sign language to communicate with her family (below, Helen with her governess, Anne Sullivan).

She certainly broke the mold by being the first deaf-blind person to graduate from college. She wrote 12 books, lectured and toured with a vaudeville act, made a movie and traveled worldwide to raise funds for the blind.

"I long to accomplish a great and noble task, but it is my chief duty to accomplish small tasks as if they were great and noble." – Helen Keller (1880-1968)

What kinds of issues are played out on Earth? Wendy Kennedy ("The Great Human Potential") explained we are here to co-create situations, where we can resolve one or more major issues that deal with a handful of *core issues*: safety, security, control, manipulation, trust, approval or abandonment. We resolve things by viewing them from another perspective.

If we're coming to experience life as a disabled person, we usually make a soul agreement with another soul, who will play the role of our caretaker. For example, Helen Keller became deaf and blind as a child, but her governess (Anne Sullivan) was her companion for 39 years. Anne was visually impaired herself. Their souls had shared several lifetimes together as sisters, inventors and other roles.

They made a great team on a path of achievement and accomplishment based on friendship and trust. Helen's life theme of service was about betterment of society by guiding others, while engaging adversity as a means to self-discovery. Anne was her trustworthy counselor, advocate, promoter, teacher and nurturer, who was realistic, accommodating, and calm, but also meant to grow through disruptions of all kinds in her life. They helped each other grow as souls.

Physicist Stephen Hawking was another role model for disabled people. At age 21, he was diagnosed with a slowly progressing neurodegenerative disease (ALS or amyotrophic lateral sclerosis) and was given two years to live. His life story was told in the film, *"A Theory of Everything."* He became gradually paralyzed and used a wheelchair with a computer and voice synthesizer to communicate with others (below).

He continued to work, write books, travel and received numerous honors in his lifetime. He became a celebrity/pop icon, who appeared in film and TV.

His life plan was very interesting. His past life issues were about giving up, playing it too safe, fearing the unknown or not taking risks. This time he was born with the Card of Fate, which meant letting go of a certain lifestyle, developing detachment and a more universal approach to life, which he did as a cosmologist. His life theme was about penetrating life on many levels. He had great ambition, an inner drive to move ahead no matter what it took with determination, practicality, power and influence. His learning came through overcoming obstacles of all kinds.

He was twice married, had three children and a number of devoted caretakers that included his wives, nurses, students and personal assistants who looked after him 24/7. His lesson was to learn to trust others with his survival, to surrender with grace, to give and receive love, and overcome his fear of rejection or uncertainty about love along with his past life tendency to manipulate and control others with love. Like Nikola Tesla, he was intuitive, imaginative and connected to the universal core for information, but remained an atheist until his death in 2018.

"There is no heaven or afterlife for broken down computers; that is a fairy story for people afraid of the dark." — Stephen Hawking (1942-2018)

People who don't believe in the afterlife may find themselves in limbo or "nothingness" just as they had imagined, but also confused by their now healthy (not disabled) body, thoughts, memories and perceptions that continue after death. Their consciousness stays dimmed until they are awakened by their guide and helpers to move on to other energetic realms and eventually to their Higher Self for a full life review (see "Spiritual Guide To Our Afterlife").

What are some lessons learned through disability? The **parent** or **caretaker** of a disabled child may be learning about themes of health issues, patience, tolerance, innocence, forgiveness, protection, sacrifice, resolve, support, unconditional love and giving, compassion, perseverance, and awareness of and adaptability to other people's needs, etc.

The **disabled person** may be learning about trust, approval, partnership, self-mastery, self-love, simplification, experimentation, choice, usefulness, stability, release, humor, cooperation, physical limitation, self-restraint, withdrawal, recuperation from exhaustion, etc.

Clinical psychologist Doris E. Cohen, PhD ("Repetition") described the complex dynamics in a family with a disabled child. The parents may be either drawn closer together or pulled apart by a child with severe or chronic physical or mental problems. The entire family is affected. Parents that have to attend to the needs of a disabled child (e.g. multiple surgeries) may be giving less attention to the siblings, who end up feeling abandoned, neglected or develop their own issues (e.g. lack of approval, anxiety, learning disability, low self-esteem, etc.). Parents that lose a child may be overwhelmed with grief, guilt or blame and very often end up divorced, which affects the surviving siblings as well.

What's the point? Guy Needler said our experience is more profound when we're incarnate, because all of us are in essence "deaf, dumb and blind" on multiple levels, because of our very tenuous connection to our Higher Self (Chapter 1). That is particularly true of our human incarnations in these very dense physical forms in the lowest frequency environment in the universe. It's like moving slowly through molasses compared to the energetic side.

If you add to that state some sensory or physical challenges, you've got an even more profound state of being, which is unlike anything we experience in the higher energetic realms. If you imagine a person, who has no sense of sight, touch, taste, smell, or hearing, and they have to exist, understand and experience life, their level of understanding and experience is going to be more profound than somebody who has those senses, because it's easier for them.

He said it's a bit like having to drive a car, but at best having somebody to tell you how to drive, where to drive, when to push the breaks, when to turn right, etc. That level of experience requires you to trust somebody else, trust those around you to work with you.

This experiential difference between having senses and no senses makes us *gain evolutionary content* much faster, when we have a lifetime with a disability of one kind or another. Ultimately, it helps us all evolve. As Ram Dass put it: "We're all just walking each other Home."

Disabled doesn't mean unable!

"Bless every person and condition, and give thanks. For nothing happens by accident in God's world, and there is no such thing as coincidence. Nor is the world buffeted by random choice, or something you call fate." — Neale Donald Walsch

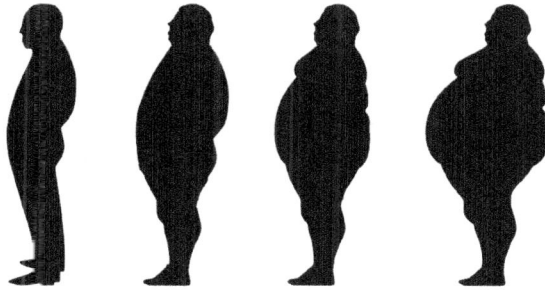

CHAPTER 5

WHAT IS THE ENERGETIC BASIS OF OBESITY?

The prevalence of obesity has nearly tripled between 1975 and 2016. About 2 billion people are overweight (defined as a body mass index or BMI of 25-29) and one third of them (over 650 million) are obese (BMI>30). Obesity is a global epidemic that impacts both adults and children in developed and developing countries.

What is the physical basis of obesity? For the past fifty years, we have been told to eat less and move more to lose weight. Cut your calories, cut the fat and watch your portion size. How is that calorie restriction working for us? Not very well. Scientists have projected that in the U.S. over 85% of adults will be obese or overweight by 2030. Obesity in children and adolescents is also increasing worldwide, wherever the western diet has been adopted.

Jason Fung, MD ("The Obesity Code") explained that the old "calories-in, calories-out" formula is way too simplistic. Obesity is a disease of *hormonal imbalance* rather than caloric imbalance. That's why it is closely related to type 2 diabetes (Chapter 6).

Our bodies have multiple overlapping systems of body weight control. They include many hormones that control hunger or tell us when we are full and should stop eating or tell the body how to distribute energy for body heat, to form new tissues, repair them, and other functions.

There are many **risk factors** for obesity that include individual (e.g. genetics, some endocrine diseases or drugs, etc.), socioeconomic and environmental factors (e.g. endocrine disrupting chemicals). They're part of the story, but not the whole story, as noted by Diet Doctor (website)

*"The **food industry** profits from selling cheap, low-fat, highly processed, nutritionally depleted and addictive food. And we're advised to eat at least every three hours.*

*The **pharmaceutical industry** profits by selling daily medications to temporarily reduce the symptoms of all the diseases caused by the food. These are trillion dollar industries."*

No wonder we get sick and tired of being sick and tired. There is a lot of money to be made by keeping us sick. Both my husband and I worked as research scientists to develop anti-obesity drugs in biopharmaceutical companies — one drug is on the market, the other is not. Both drugs were based on the wrong mechanism of action. We know more about metabolic diseases now.

*"**We can no longer view different disease states as distinct biochemical entities.** Nearly all degenerative diseases have the same underlying biochemical etiology — that is a **diet-induced pro-inflammatory state.** Although specific diseases may require specific treatments such as beta blockers for hypertension, chemotherapy for cancer, the treatment program must also include nutritional*

protocols to reduce the pro-inflammatory state." — Bruce Hoffman, MD (Instagram@drbrucehoffman)

Obesity and type 2 diabetes are just the tip of the iceberg followed by other conditions associated with **metabolic disease**, such as heart and vascular diseases, hypertension, dyslipidemia, many cancers, food addiction, osteoarthritis, infertility, sleep apnea, asthma, gallstones, fatty liver disease, stroke, Alzheimer's disease, etc.

These conditions are just different manifestations of the same underlying metabolic disease. They add up to skyrocketing medical costs that will bankrupt our health care systems worldwide. They mean shorter and poorer quality lifespans for all of us. We can do better.

What's the solution? We are not to blame for the condition we are in. We have been given poor dietary guidelines and misguided medical advice for five decades, such as eat three meals a day with snacks, eat a low fat diet, avoid eggs, but take a statin drug for life to lower your cholesterol — despite the findings that show statin use makes no difference in the risk of cardiovascular disease, but is clearly linked to developing type 2 diabetes (especially in women) and cognitive decline or dementia. The older you are, the worse the side effects of statins are.

There is no one-size-fits-all solution to anything in health and medicine. Diets and medicines that work for some people don't work for others or may cause serious side effects in them. Why? Everybody has a different lifestyle, diet and metabolic profile, different energetic blueprint, genetics, epigenetics and pharmacogenetics, which determines how your DNA responds to drugs or any toxic chemicals in the environment (e.g. food, water, air, soil, etc.).

If you are overweight or obese, the doctor usually puts the blame on you, not the western or Standard American Diet ("SAD") that consists of pre-packaged, processed or fast food made of meat fried in pro-inflammatory oils with a side of refined carbohydrates (e.g. bread, pasta, rice, potatoes) and supersized drinks with added sugar or high fructose corn syrup (below).

It's *addictive* to both adults and children, who get 60-70% of all calories from ultra-processed foods made from commodity crops like corn, wheat and soybeans (e.g. packaged chips, crackers, bread, breakfast cereal, cake mixes, donuts, candy, soft drinks, chicken nuggets, pizza, hotdogs, ready to eat rice or pasta dishes, etc.).

These highly processed foods occupy the largest area (usually the middle aisles) of every grocery store. No wonder we get sick! Our high carbohydrate, highly inflammatory diet is responsible for about 11 million deaths every year worldwide.

Functional medicine doctor Mark Hyman, MD, said one hundred years ago we didn't need labels to tell us our food was local, organic or grass-fed. All food was whole, unadulterated and real. We have lost our connection to our food and think there is a "pill for every ill."

*"**Food** isn't like medicine, it is medicine. Food has the power to heal. Food is the most powerful drug on the planet. It can improve the expression of thousands of genes, balance dozens of hormones, optimize tens of thousands of protein networks, reduce inflammation, and optimize your microbiome (gut flora). Focus on eating nutrient dense whole foods that fuel your body and don't spike your blood sugar."* — Mark Hyman, MD (Instagram@drmarkhyman)

Jason Fung, MD, sees a lot of obese and diabetic patients whose kidney function is impaired. He prescribes the oldest lifestyle intervention known to humans, which is **fasting** combined with a **low-carbohydrate diet.** The goal is to put less sugar less often into the body and to burn it off with "intermittent fasting" or "time restricted eating."

Why? He said a dietary disease requires a dietary treatment, because you cannot exercise your way out of a bad diet. It is scientifically proven that high carb diets impair fat cells from burning energy. That's what we want to avoid, as it favors fat storage rather than fat burning.

Dr. Hyman said belly fat (visceral fat around the organs) is the #1 cause of aging. Why? It produces *inflammatory cytokines* (e.g. tumor necrosis factor, interleukin 6) that drive **chronic inflammation** in the body. That increases the risk of blood clots, changes your hormones and brain chemistry and more. These doctors hope we can eradicate obesity, diabetes, dementia and chronic diseases within a generation with diet, lifestyle modification and intermittent fasting.

*"**Fasting** is a great way to optimize your health...it is a **free tool** that activates all the systems in your body to protect you, heal you, and help you live longer. Fasting can help to reduce inflammation, brain fog, and insulin*

resistance. It can also increase energy and bone density and activate autophagy, which is the process of cleaning out damaged cells." — Mark Hyman, MD

How to start fasting? In practice, **fasting** means eating in a *window* of 1-12 hrs and fasting the rest of the day and night when we're sleeping. There are many types of fasting windows. Nobody eats while they are sleeping, so everybody should be able to do a 12 hr eating window.

First, you may need to remove processed foods from your diet to get you primed for fasting. Eat whole foods prepared by you at home, so you know exactly what you're eating. Then you can try a 10 hr or 8 hr eating window (eat 2-3 meals in that period) and fast the rest of the day. You can drink liquids, like water, coffee, tea, bone broth as needed during the fasting period.

You could do the 8/16 for a week or two. Then try a shorter eating window, e.g. 6/18, 4/20 ("warrior diet"), or 1/23 ("OMAD" or one-meal-a-day) for another week or two. By three weeks, you will have reprogrammed your body — your **food addiction** and **hunger** pangs are gone!

Most people start fasting to get rapid but healthy **weight loss** or to **reverse a disease**, such as obesity, diabetes or *metabolic syndrome* (combination of obesity, type 2 diabetes, hypertension, and cardiovascular disease). **All these conditions can be *reversed* with intermittent fasting.**

This is a paradigm shifting approach, which is not as difficult it sounds. It's not a diet, it's a lifestyle. Fasting is not the same as starvation at all. It may take a few weeks to adapt to fasting by gradually shortening the window to eat two meals a day within an 8 hr or 6 hr or 4 hr or 2 hr window or whatever suits your lifestyle. Once established as a daily routine, it can be continued safely for many years. You can listen to your body and stick to a window that works best for your work schedule and family life, since everybody's life is different.

Just for reference, my husband has been doing OMAD for 12 years now and has never been fitter or healthier (see Juan Sarmiento - YouTube or his website: FeastFastForLife.com, below). He does raised push-ups at home for muscle building and maintenance. No gym, supplements or other gimmicks are needed (below).

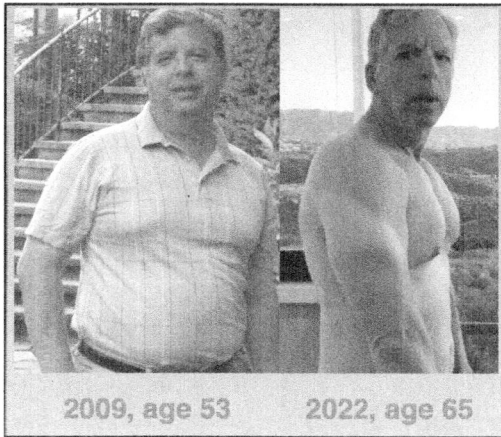

2009, age 53   2022, age 65

When we get older, we tend to develop *sarcopenia* or progressive loss of muscle mass and function, which contributes to muscle weakness, disability, frailty, falling and fractures. It is preventable and reversible with **regular exercise**, such as calisthenics, which involves stretching and muscle strength training by doing push-ups (against the wall, stairs, floor, etc.), planks, pull-ups, sit-ups (whatever you're capable of doing) — not for hours like a body builder, but even 5-10 minutes a day is better than nothing — better than a fractured hip and hospitalization.

At first, fasting may sound crazy or too extreme, but newer scientific findings back up our experience. **Fasting is a metabolic workout and an anti-aging treatment at the same time!** It repairs damaged cells and tissues (by autophagy and mitophagy) and rejuvenates the whole body.

I have been fasting daily (2/22 or 3/21) for almost four years. As the body adapts to fasting, weight loss happens naturally. My husband lost 60 lbs and I lost 30 lbs until we reached a body weight that was healthy and sustainable. Whatever metabolic diseases we had before are gone!

Fasting is different from the *ketogenic diet,* which is a strict low-carb (<20 g/day), high-fat diet to induce ketosis for quick weight loss and other therapeutic reasons (e.g. obesity, diabetes, epilepsy, liver transplant, metabolic psychiatry for schizophrenia, bipolar disorder, etc.). People on the keto diet eat three meals a day, so they don't do any fasting. They measure their ketone levels in blood or urine and often cannot sustain the diet for more than 3-6 months. They get sick of eating the same foods or give it up when their weight plateaus, so they go back to old habits.

The difference with fasting is we can eat whatever we want and don't ever count calories or measure ketone levels. People often ask us, what *do* you eat? Here are some homemade dishes suited for a fasting lifestyle, such as soups, breads, cheeses, salads, vegetable casseroles and a variety of delicious homemade low-carb desserts (below). You can find fasting guidelines and thousands of free low-carb recipes online (e.g. DietDoctor.com).

We *exercise* in the morning in the *fasting state*, when we have the most energy to walk, hike, do push-ups or whatever. The exercise (e.g. hiking) allows you to eat high quality, nutrient dense foods every day without lowering your resting metabolic rate, which may happen with dieting or calorie restriction. We cook all our own meals from fresh, whole foods, and *eat to satiety* around lunch and fast the rest of the day. We do it every day of the week — we don't believe in "cheat days," because they will just bring back your hunger pangs. Consistency is the key.

It is important to eat a high-protein diet (e.g. 90 g/women; 110 g/men) and add *resistance training* to help maintain lean muscle mass. One-meal-a-day is not for everyone, but it saves us a lot of time in shopping, cooking and cleaning, because we skip breakfast and dinner.

The best part is that we have *extra energy* for all kinds of physical and mental activities (e.g. learning new languages, writing books, creating YouTube videos, etc.), because our bodies have made a "metabolic switch" to become fat-adapted and use *ketone bodies* (actually preferred by your brain, heart, muscles, etc.) rather than glucose as the primary fuel.

We don't feel hungry, deprived or restricted in any way, which makes this regimen sustainable for life. **We believe this is the way humans will eat in the future — less food and less often.**

This translates to fewer insulin spikes and less inflammation, which will *reverse* and/or *prevent* many of the chronic diseases that reduce the overall quality of life in elderly people. It will also help to reduce the cost and burden of healthcare in western countries. We owe it to ourselves and our children to *take responsibility* of our own health and well-being.

What is the energetic basis of obesity? Here is a brief summary of the work of Wendy Kennedy, Louise Hay, Anodea Judith, Karen Curry and Guy Needler — each adding their own perspective to the energetic basis of obesity and body issues, physical health and well-being.

There are **four main factors** that influence our choices around food, nutrition and wellness:

1. Energy protection: Carrying extra weight or fat is a level of protection for those who are fearful, not feeling safe in their body. There are several markers in the soul blueprint to consider.

Some people with **Gate 19** (Sensitivity/Attunement) are highly attuned and hypersensitive to the emotional energies and shifts around them, such as food changes, textures (sensitive palate), clothing, and other environmental conditions. They are also naturally attuned and very sensitive to animals (e.g. animal "whisperers"). They may prefer to become vegetarians, which is our destiny as we shift and evolve as a species.

People with "open" lower chakras (first, second, third and fourth) pick up and amplify the energies, feelings, fears, pressures or pains of those around them. They may try to block it off by carrying extra weight (e.g. belly fat) or by unconsciously protecting their chakras with a haze of energy, cling film, spikes or other means that may interfere with the function of those chakras, as noted by Guy Needler ("Psycho-Spiritual Healing").

Some people also have certain energy channels (e.g. Channels of Community, Connecting, Preservation, Emoting and Sensitivity) that connect their lower chakras in a way to make them associate the energy of food as the energy of love, belonging and community. If they don't feel loved or like they belong, they try to sustain themselves by getting that energy from food.

Similarly, people that feel emptiness, separation, lack of energy or lack of abundance in life associated with **Gate 55** (Abundant Spirit) may overcompensate by overeating, which may affect their pancreas (e.g. type 2 diabetes). To heal our relationship to food, we have to start by healing our connection to Source and trust that we are supported even when we are *fasting*.

Finally, people with **Gate 30** (Desires/Intensity) may be ultra-intense or not living a balanced life, which often leads to *burnout*. They may be pushing too hard or too fast, going in the wrong direction or trying to be something that they are not (e.g. people pleaser, inauthentic self, etc.).

2. Conditioning: Genetics is one part of our conditioning and also plays a role in some forms of obesity. Imprinting from the family of origin is the most common way we are conditioned by our parents and culture. Their eating, behavior patterns and attitudes toward food and body image may strongly influence us for better or worse growing up.

"Diet is what runs in the family, not diseases. Change your diet and you will escape your family history of diseases. Remember genes predispose but do not predetermine." — *Dr. James DiNicolantonio ("The Longevity Solution")*

Intergenerational family dynamics (Chapter 9) also create *epigenetic influences* on gene expression that affect our health and well-being. When we heal ourselves, we impact our family in multiple generations — those that came before us and those that will come after us. You can be a generational pattern shifter (see "Spiritual Guide To Our Awakening").

3. Coping with unmet needs: We are designed to give and take energy, and we all have a unique set of energy needs that seek fulfillment in life. If our energy needs are not being met, we develop various *coping strategies* from childhood onwards. Obesity may arise from an imbalance in the lower three chakras that support our gross physical form (at FB 1-3).

When the *first chakra* is excessive, we may eat too much and gain weight to create more body mass to ground or anchor us in the world. We may also become fixated on money or materialism via **Gate 54** (Greed/Ambition) or hoarding via **Gate 39** (Hardship/Obstacles), because we are focused on safety and survival issues and fear change.

We may need to dissipate the energy of fighting with life via **Gate 38** (Fighter/Opposition) in favor of growing in life via **Gate 53** (New Beginnings) to transcend our limitations via **Gate 60** (Resourcefulness/Self-Restraint). All these gates and their self-preservation influences are found in the root or first chakra.

When the *second chakra* is excessive, we may be fixated on cooking and eating comfort foods or snacking as a substitute for emotional nurturing via **Gate 27** (Nurturing/Nourishing) or bonding via **Gate 59** (Sexuality/Intimacy) that was lacking in our family or tribe. Although we may feel lethargic or reluctant to move out of safe patterns via **Gate 9** (Inertia/Diversion), a heavy body gives us a sense of support via **Gate 29** (Devotion/Commitment) and solidity in life via **Gate 5** (Daily Rituals, like snacks), **Gate 14** (Harvesting) and **Gate 34** (Outer Strength).

When the *third chakra* is blocked from expressing anger, the charge builds up in the body as a metabolic defect. It may manifest as being overweight or obese through various

energy channels that connect the root to the third chakra. This figure illustrates some of the channels that may be influencing our weight issues for different reasons or motivations (below).

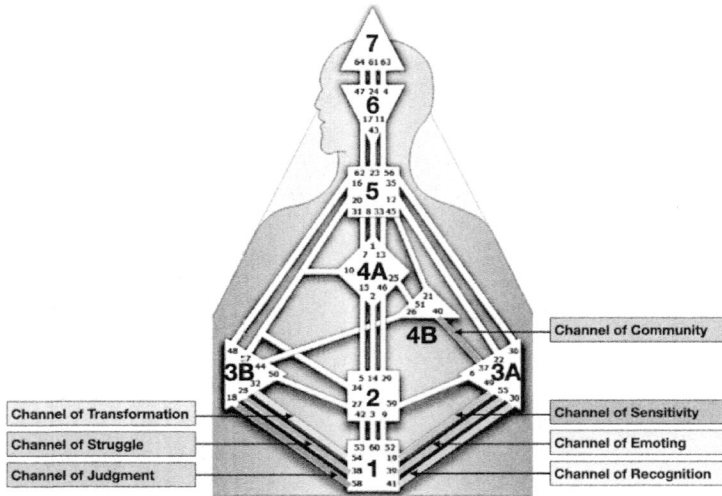

You may have conflicting energies (both attraction and repulsion) at two ends of the channel, that are difficult to navigate at the lower end of expression, creating unmet needs. For example, you may have the entire channel in your own blueprint or play it out with someone around you (e.g. parent, partner, friend), who completes the channel with you — you may have one end of it and they have the other end, which creates "sparks" in that energy channel for both of you. How?

Here are some thoughts, behaviors and actions associated with different channels:

The first four channels are driven by *feeling* in the **solar plexus chakra (chakra 3A):**

Oversensitivity may arise via the **Channel of Sensitivity** that connects **Gate 19** of Inclusion with **Gate 49** of Rejection. At one end of the channel, the person may feel isolated, needy or codependent and wants to be included, while the other end may be emotionally nervous and afraid of being rejected, so they may react against others before getting rejected themselves.

Moodiness may arise via the **Channel of Emoting** between **Gate 39** of Hoarding/Hardship and **Gate 55** of Lack Mentality/Emptiness, which can lead to hoarding of food or overeating because of the mood to eat or feeling of emptiness inside.

Cravings may arise via the **Channel of Recognition of Feelings**, which includes hunger that runs between **Gate 30** of Intense Needs/Desires/Cravings and **Gate 41** of Anticipation, which wants to fantasize or wait until the time is right. The two are at odds with each other. Cravings often win.

Aloneness may arise via the **Channel of Community** between **Gate 37** of Friends/Family (chakra 3A) and **Gate 40** of Love of Work/Exhaustion/Aloneness (chakra 4B). This channel is meant to sustain our tribal food stores in lean and fat years. To maintain balance, we need to work together as a tribe, but also take time to rest and have some alone time to stay healthy. When we lose our connection to our family/tribe, we may feel alone and reach for food and overeat to fulfill that unmet need for interacting with family, friends, and community.

The next three channels are driven by *fear* in the **splenic chakra (chakra 3B):**

Judgment may arise via the **Channel of Judgment** that connects **Gate 18** of Judgment (e.g. self-judgment) with

Gate 58 of Dissatisfaction (e.g. joyless life), which creates a conundrum.

Fighting with life may arise via the **Channel of Struggle** that runs between **Gate 38** of The Stubborn Fighter and **Gate 28** of The Risk Taker, which can lead to outbursts or feelings of futility. These gates are meant to act as a catalyst for change, not to bring you pain and suffering.

Conflict may also arise via the **Channel of Transformation** between **Gate 54** of Material Ambition that is driven to achieve (e.g. greed for food, drinking) and **Gate 32** of Conservation that has a fear of failure and wants to preserve things as is.

You can see the interplay of attracting and opposing energies in all these channels that may contribute to our sensitivity, moods, cravings, overeating, hoarding, fighting, greed, etc.

The *third chakra* may also be associated with a **digestive disorder** (e.g. inflammatory bowel disease, gut microbiome imbalance, pro-inflammatory diet, leaky gut, food intolerance, etc.). When the food we eat is not digested, absorbed or assimilated properly into the cells that need it, it will not give us enough energy, because it's not processed properly. We reach for more food, but get frustrated by more abdominal pain and discomfort after eating.

Normally, the parasympathetic response is to *rest and digest* after eating, which is the opposite of the *fight and flight* response of the sympathetic nervous system. Both are part of the **enteric nervous system** that controls the gastrointestinal tract. It is called our "**second brain**," because it operates autonomously, but also communicates with the central nervous system (brain/spinal cord) via the *gut-brain axis*. That explains why our metabolism often improves, when the anger and frustration is released (via psycho-spiritual programming and other means).

The gastrointestinal tract has many functions, such as ingestion of food and water, physical and chemical digestion, absorption of nutrients and water, and then elimination of undigested waste products (below).

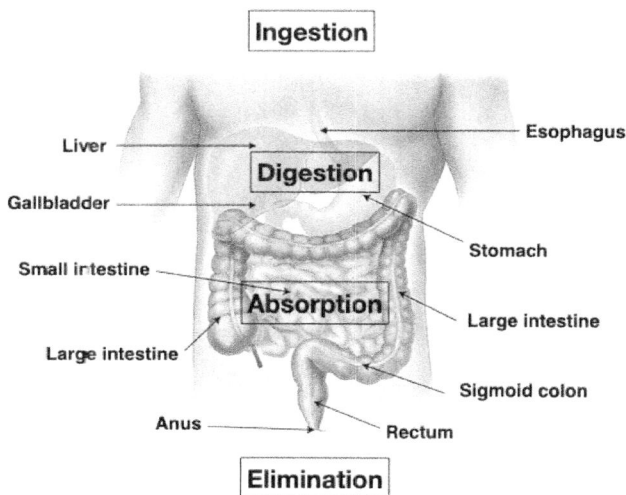

There are many gates assigned to eating, absorption, digestion and elimination functions, such as hunger recognition (Gate 30), wave of hunger (Gate 36), mood to eat (Gate 55), impulse to eat (Gate 39), mouth (Gate 37), stomach (Gate 40), liver (Gate 15), gallbladder (Gate 51), small intestine (Gate 14), pH balance (Gate 6), fullness (Gate 35), colon (Gate 60), etc.

These gates remind us of the numerous signals that govern various physiologic functions in our body. These gates and channels don't doom us with their low expression for life. We use them to experience certain states of "beingness" for ourselves. They serve to bring about change.

Every gate has a gift for us — it's built-in to our blueprint and we just need to express it. For example, Gate 19 (Sensitivity) has the gift of exquisite attunement to people and animals around you. Gate 38 (Fighter) gives you the ability to stand in your power and fight for what is right. Gate 18 (Judgment) gives you the integrity to know what is correct (or not) and what needs to be improved. Gate 40 brings you resolve and freedom to act by your own will or Higher will, etc.

4. Belief systems: We live in a society with many negative or distorted belief systems about food, nutrition, body image, shape and size. We are bombarded by idealized (or digitally altered) body images and mixed messages that make regular people feel unattractive or defective. We may become insecure about our body and develop self-rejection of one or more parts of us.

Your physical body is a reflection of your energetic state. Wendy Kennedy ("The Great Human Potential") said if your thoughts or *beliefs* are negative (e.g. your body is flawed or broken), then the body will honor that to give the illusion that something is broken. Then you may work on some physical ailment for a while until you shift your beliefs.

On the other hand, if you *accept* your body, appreciate it for all the mileage it has given you, and know that you are perfectly beautiful exactly as you are, your body will start to respond to that new belief — to find a natural balance and crave foods that are healthier and more nutritious.

You may start to move your body more, to ground yourself to the Earth, to feel more balanced and supported by life. That's the path of transformation from self-hatred and self-rejection to *self-love* and *self-acceptance* that leads to health and well-being.

What's the point? There is no one-size-fits-all approach to food, nutrition, health and wellness. When Guy Needler was asked why we're having this epidemic of overweight and obese people in our society, he said *it's all about experience.* It's a piece of **psycho-spiritual programming** that is part of our **life plan** — we do it to understand and experience certain physical conditions in more detail by experiencing them personally.

When we are disincarnate, our souls often choose things that we don't like as human beings, because it doesn't hold the same level of abhorrence to us in the energetic realm. Anything that gives us a chance to learn, experience and maybe overcome something is ultimately for our soul's evolution. But everybody has their own path to navigate.

There are some people, who want to experience different diseases or psychological or psycho-spiritual conditions. They intend to experience them full stop and not overcome them, so they allow themselves to go through a downward spiral with them. Other individuals may want to overcome the condition and stay as they are, or heal and move upwards in life. All is choice.

He said recently we have been dropping down in our frequency as a collective. People in a low frequency environment want a quick fix, like a pill or fast food, processed food, anything to soothe or numb themselves. It's the quick and easy way of doing things, according to Needler.

The best approach is not drugs (e.g. diet pills) or surgery (e.g. gastric bypass), but a mixture of psycho-spiritual healing, which means spiritual counseling and energy healing. The objective is to change the psycho-spiritual programming, so that the person starts to change the way they think, behave and act in terms of the energies gained through eating physical foods.

All healing begins with *choosing to heal* — it takes both inner and outer work to follow through with it. Just know that all of us are works in progress — no exceptions.

"To heal is to touch with love that which we previously touched with fear." — Stephen Levine

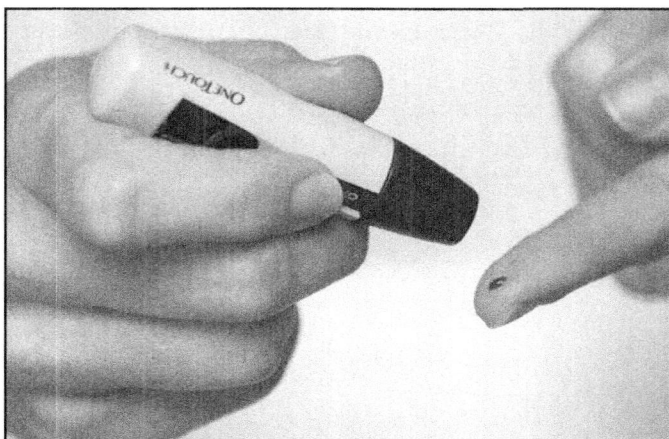

CHAPTER 6

WHAT IS THE ENERGETIC BASIS OF DIABETES?

This chapter is a companion to Chapter 5 on Obesity, which is closely related to Diabetes. We have come to understand that the two conditions are really one and the same disease, which some call "**Diabesity**" to reflect the relationship between Diabetes and Obesity.

What is the physical basis of diabetes? The prevalence of diabetes has quadrupled in the past three decades. About 1 in 11 adults worldwide now have diabetes, which is the ninth major cause of death. It is another global epidemic, like obesity.

While being overweight or obese is easy to diagnose, **diabetes** and its predecessor, which is called **prediabetes** are more insidious, because they require a blood sugar test for diagnosis. In the U.S., more than 50% of people have type 2 diabetes (T2D) or prediabetes with higher than normal blood sugar levels, but 9 out of 10 prediabetics don't know it. Even one out of four diabetics don't know that they have a chronic disease that is progressive, if left untreated. Here is a figure that illustrates the main symptoms of Type 1 and Type 2 Diabetes (below).

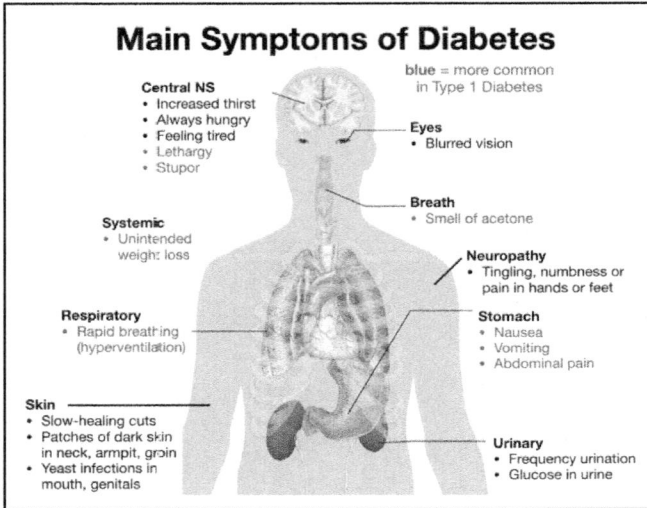

Main Symptoms of Diabetes

blue = more common in Type 1 Diabetes

Central NS
• Increased thirst
• Always hungry
• Feeling tired
• Lethargy
• Stupor

Eyes
• Blurred vision

Breath
• Smell of acetone

Systemic
• Unintended weight loss

Neuropathy
• Tingling, numbness or pain in hands or feet

Respiratory
• Rapid breathing (hyperventilation)

Stomach
• Nausea
• Vomiting
• Abdominal pain

Skin
• Slow-healing cuts
• Patches of dark skin in neck, armpit, groin
• Yeast infections in mouth, genitals

Urinary
• Frequency urination
• Glucose in urine

Diabetes is a disease of hormonal imbalance. About 90-95% of diabetics have *too much* insulin **(type 2 diabetes)**, whereas 10% of diabetics have *too little* insulin **(type 1 diabetes)**. They are polar opposites that require different cures, according to Jason Fung, MD ("The Diabetes Code"), who is a nephrologist that sees lots of diabetics with kidney disease.

He said for the first time in history more people have the disease than not! Since it affects both sexes, every age group, every racial and ethnic group and all education levels, it's not genetics or part of the normal aging process, it's a lifestyle issue related to our *food intake.*

Obesity typically precedes the diagnosis of diabetes by a decade or more. Even a small weight gain increases the risk of type 2 diabetes. Dr. Fung said it takes just 11 lbs extra weight to up the risk by 90% and anything over 18 lbs ups it by 270%. Why?

Obese people develop a *fatty liver*, which is the first step toward diabetes. It only takes three weeks of overeating sugary snacks to develop a fatty liver. Similarly, after just one week of overeating fructose, you get *insulin resistance* (where your cells resist or ignore the insulin signal to absorb glucose from your blood, so you get higher than normal blood sugar levels). Then in eight weeks, you're *prediabetic* (with fasting blood glucose of 100-126 mg/dl or HbA1c of 5.7-6.4%).

That's alarmingly fast! Fatty liver is reversible, but overeating sugar and starches (e.g. rice, corn, wheat, potatoes, etc.) over time leads to a high blood sugar level and a high blood insulin level, insulin resistance in the liver (where the cells can't take up glucose from blood for energy) and fatty infiltration of muscle, pancreas and other tissues. Things just get worse from there on!

Too much belly fat in the abdomen and around the visceral organs is the main cause of insulin resistance or *metabolic syndrome* (combination of obesity, type 2 diabetes, hypertension, and cardiovascular disease), which affects 10-84% of the population depending on the country.

Type 2 diabetes affects every organ in the body. The complications include blindness, kidney disease, nerve damage, atherosclerosis, heart disease, stroke, cancer, infections, erectile dysfunction, polycystic ovarian syndrome and Alzheimer's disease (called **type 3 diabetes**).

The overall impact of these conditions is high medical costs, lower quality of life and shorter lifespans. After you are diagnosed as having prediabetes, your doctor usually prescribes one or more **prescription drugs** for life to try to control your high blood glucose, high cholesterol, high blood pressure along with a low-fat, low-calorie diet, exercise and maybe bariatric surgery, if you're morbidly obese (BMI>40). Do they work?

Do prescription drugs work? Dr. Fung described a clinical trial on superobese type 2 diabetics that compared the effects of **gastric bypass surgery** with intensive **drug treatments**. The results were clear. The drug treatments didn't really work. The diabetics had to have larger doses of multiple drugs, including insulin. Even so they just got worse, sicker and fatter.

In contrast, about 95% of those that had the bypass surgery reversed their diabetes within weeks of surgery, long before they lost much weight. They became *nondiabetic*. Why? The surgery induced a sudden, severe caloric restriction. This forced them to burn fat for energy.

Within three months, most of them had stopped taking their diabetic medications but kept losing weight, and their blood glucose stayed normal for ten years. But this surgery has some drawbacks, including excess skin folds, nutritional deficiencies over time (e.g. iron, calcium, vitamin B1/B12), risk of gallstones, stomach ulcers, hypoglycemia, and weight re-gain.

Does liposuction work the same way? No, because it just removes some fat, but doesn't give any metabolic benefit. It's all cosmetic, not fat burning.

Why don't more diabetics have surgery? Because surgery is not the answer for many reasons. It is costly and has some complications, including the loss of some hormones secreted by a healthy stomach. Besides, now we know how get the same benefits without surgery.

Dr. Fung prescribes a new way to REVERSE type 2 diabetes using these steps:

Eat a low-carbohydrate, healthy-fat (LCHF) diet by reducing the intake of refined carbohydrates and by using natural healthy fats (e.g. avocado, olive oil, nuts, fish, eggs, etc.). The amount of daily net carbs may range from liberal (50-100 g) to moderate (20-50 g) to strict ketogenic diet (<20 g), compared to most western diets that have >250 g net carbs/day.

Note: *Total carbs* include all types of carbs in a food, including starches, fiber and sugar. *Net carbs* only include the carbs that the body can digest into glucose. To calculate net carbs, use this formula: Net carbs = Total carbs - Fiber. The fiber isn't digested into glucose.

Avoid fructose (e.g. table sugar, high-fructose corn syrup, foods with added or hidden sugars) and certain artificial sweeteners that tend to raise insulin levels as well (e.g. maltitol, xylitol, dextrose, saccharin, aspartame, Splenda, Equal, Sweet'N Low, Stevia-in-the-Raw).

Also avoid white sugar, brown sugar, maple syrup, coconut sugar, dates, honey, corn syrup, agave syrup, and fruit juices. Some sugar substitutes can be used in baking (e.g. pure Stevia, erythritol, Truvia, monk fruit) to create low-carb versions of your favorite desserts (Chapter 5).

Eat real food prepared at home, not refined or processed or packaged or fast foods. It's easy to adjust most recipes by using vegetables, nut flours, flaxseed, chia seeds, etc. You don't need to feel deprived or miss out on anything worth putting into your body.

Use intermittent fasting adjusted to your lifestyle (e.g. fast 24 hrs three times a week, or eat during a 1-to-8 hr-window and fast the rest of the day). The goal is to reduce the number of *insulin spikes* in a day. Fasting is flexible and free. It keeps your basal metabolism high, because fasting is not the same as starvation or a low calorie diet.

The body soon becomes "fat adapted" to use your own body fat and dietary fat for fuel. It is a "metabolic switch" from glucose to ketone bodies. It is not a diet, it's a lifestyle modification for longevity and vitality. Work with a health care professional to do it safely and properly, especially if you are on any prescription medications.

Exercise is an added bonus to burn off remaining fat and sugar (e.g. walking, hiking, tennis, yoga, aerobics, calisthenics, swimming, etc.). It's also of benefit to your brain function.

If you don't have enough energy, you need to find ways to generate it. Anodea Judith ("Charge and the Energy Body") recommends a good diet, breath work, movement and rest as needed. Exercise stimulates metabolism by generating energy and moving the charge trapped in the body. The body becomes more fit and efficient.

Dr. Fung said both intermittent fasting and low-carbohydrate, healthy-fat (LCHF) diets effectively reduce insulin, and thus can cause weight loss and reverse type 2 diabetes. He said low carb diets reduce insulin by roughly half, and fasting reduces that by another 50%. It's not a question of either/or. We need *both* fasting and a LCHF diet for maximal health benefits. Why?

Type 2 diabetes is a dietary disease, and fixing the diet will reverse the disease. It is not a cure, but it will manage the disease without medications for life (e.g. metformin, insulin, etc.).

What is the energetic basis of diabetes? Given that **diabetes** is closely related to **obesity**, the energetic factors that influence our choices around food, nutrition, health and wellness apply here as well (see Chapter 5).

In terms of our energy body, the **third chakra** is associated with energizing the stomach, liver, gallbladder, pancreas and small intestine, which digest, metabolize, absorb and assimilate nutrients in physical food. Therefore, physical malfunctions involving this chakra are seen as stomach ulcers, liver disease, gallstones, diabetes, hypoglycemia, irritable bowel disease, chronic fatigue, etc. (Chapter 5).

The third chakra is also associated with a human developmental stage, which is about the **basic right to be an individual.** It's about self-esteem, ego identity and differentiating yourself from others. Anodea Judith described what happens in a society obsessed with **power.**

People who are physically abused or traumatized in some way (e.g. authoritarianism, volatile home, shaming, etc.) don't get the respect or recognition from others to develop their own sense of personal power or confidence, so they find other ways to cope. They can underexpress their third chakra (deficient) due to fear or overexpress it (excessive) due to anger.

An **excessive third chakra** is manifest as overly aggressive, dominating or controlling behavior. The person may be power hungry, manipulative, deceitful, driven, stubborn and competitive, wanting power *over* others. They play the victimizer or persecutor role (below).

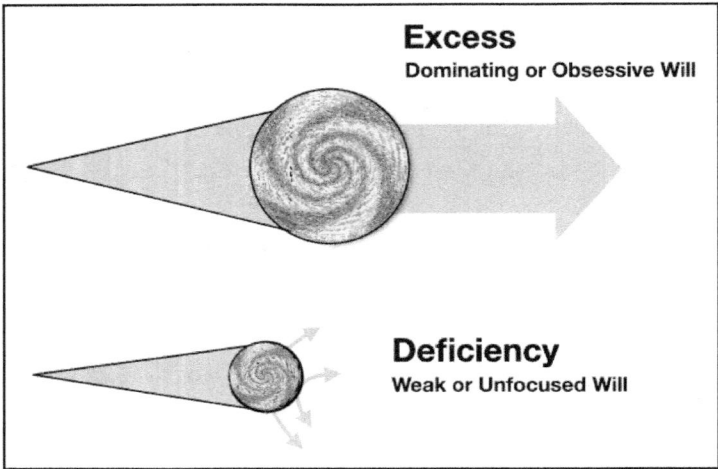

Excess
Dominating or Obsessive Will

Deficiency
Weak or Unfocused Will

A **deficient third chakra** is seen as victim mentality with low self-esteem, low energy, weak or aimless will, poor self-discipline, poor follow-through, complaining and blaming others. There is a longing for what might have been — a deep sorrow and no sweetness left in life.

In the Human Design system, the **victim/victimizer** shadow state is described by **Gate 55** (Gate of Faith/ Abundant Spirit/Lack Mentality). There is a **fear of emptiness** that can lead to potential **eating disorders**. People who feel emptiness, separation, lack of energy or lack of abundance in life may overcompensate by overeating, which affects their liver (fatty liver), pancreas (diabetes), and other organs, etc.

It may seem like a stretch to some people, but to heal our relationship to food, we have to start by healing our connection to Source/God and heal our trust in Spirit to know we are being supported at all times — even when we're fasting, for instance.

The path of growth in **Gate 55** of Faith goes from the shadow of being the victim of drama (drama happens to get your attention) to the gift of freedom from drama to the siddhi (or divine gift) of freedom that comes from the collective awakening to their Higher Selves (see "Spiritual Guide To Our Awakening"). We can awaken to be the way-showers for others.

What's the point? As Richard Rudd ("Gene Keys") wrote, our **future superfood is Love**, which is part of our spirit that is infinitely abundant in all aspects of life. It is a "want-not" state of beingness that will heal us all. But since we're not there yet, we need to keep in mind what Guy Needler recently told us about life plans.

Being overweight, obese or diabetic is all about experience. It's a piece of *psycho-spiritual programming* that is part of our life plan. We do it to understand and experience certain conditions "up close and personally." Our soul evolves from anything that gives us a chance to learn, experience and possibly overcome something.

Sometimes we want to experience different diseases or psychological or psycho-spiritual conditions just to experience them full stop and not overcome them, but go on to further decrepitude by choice. Other times we may want to experience a condition for a while, stay as we are or try to overcome it to move upwards to a healthier, more efficient state to accomplish more of what we came to do in this incarnation. All experience is valid to our Source.

We also know that all is choice — even our healing begins with choosing to heal. I hope this chapter gives you a new way to think about chronic diseases, such as diabetes and obesity, which are very prevalent in our society. We can deal with them, each in our own way, as we look at our personal and collective beliefs about Spirit, God, sustainability and faith in the abundance of life. That's the bigger picture here that is easy to miss from an earthling's point of view, who only sees the dis-ease and disease within and without.

"The human will is intensity of desire raised to the level of action." — *John Bradshaw*

CHAPTER 7

WHAT IS THE ENERGETIC BASIS OF DEMENTIA?

This is a companion to the chapters about Obesity and Diabetes, which are metabolic disease conditions that may be associated with developing Dementia later in life. The bad news is these conditions are becoming more prevalent in our busy, stressed out society that is aging. The good news is they may be preventable or reversible with newer therapeutic programs.

What is dementia vs. Alzheimer's disease? Dementia is characterized by gradual deterioration in *cognitive functions*, such as thinking, comprehension, memory, language, numbers, orientation and learning capacity along with changes in emotional control, mood and behavior. But consciousness is not affected.

Dementia results from a variety of diseases and injuries that affect the brain. There are many different forms of dementia, but Alzheimer's disease is the most common form. There are about 50 million people worldwide that have Alzheimer's or a related dementia, including Lewy body, vascular, Parkinson's, alcoholic or frontotemporal dementia. In the U.S., the proportion of people with Alzheimer's disease is 4% at < 65 yrs; 15% at 65-74 yrs; 44% at 77-84 yrs; 38% at age 85+ yrs. Life expectancy after diagnosis of Alzheimer's is 4-8 years (or longer).

One in three seniors dies with some form of dementia. By 2050, the total number of people with dementia is set to triple to 132-152 million cases worldwide. Dementia can be overwhelming for the families and caretakers in terms of physical, emotional and economic pressures. The societal costs are huge (estimated $2 trillion in 2030 in U.S. alone).

What are the risk factors? The strongest risk factor for dementia is advancing age. Other risk factors include genetics, family history, obesity, prediabetes, diabetes, hypertension, unhealthy diets (e.g. high carb), smoking, alcohol, taking statin drugs, physical and mental inactivity, lower educational level, depression and negative beliefs about aging.

Scientists have noted that the damage to the brain starts at least 20 years before any symptoms appear. It's really a disease of your 40s, 50s and 60s — it just gets diagnosed in your later years. When a person develops mild but noticeable trouble with memory, work, driving, concentration, etc., they may have mild cognitive impairment (MCI). About 38% of those with MCI (especially with memory problems) develop Alzheimer's dementia within 5 years.

The goal is to identify people at this stage (pre-dementia). Dale Bredesen, MD ("The End of Alzheimer's: The First Programme to Prevent and Reverse the Cognitive Decline of Dementia") wants to eradicate this disease. To do that, he suggested we all need a cognitive screening test ("cognoscopy") at age 45 to determine our overall health status.

How can we prevent or reverse age-related cognitive decline? The old approach to Alzheimer's was just to treat some symptoms, because the disease was deemed irreversible. All single drug therapies have failed in clinical trials, because it's not a single disease.

"Alzheimer's disease is not a mysterious, untreatable brain disease — it is reversible, metabolic/toxic, usually systemic illness with a relatively large window for treatment." — Dale Bredesen ("The End of Alzheimers")

Dr. Bredesen has pioneered a new approach to treat the underlying disease. He has described **three major subtypes of AD** identified by various blood markers and tests:

Inflammatory subtype — induced by a proinflammatory diet or infections that cause systemic inflammation, e.g. leaky gut, leaky blood-brain barrier, poor oral hygiene, chronic gingivitis, chronic sinusitis, autoimmune disease, glycated proteins in fried or processed foods, ApoE4 driving inflammation, etc.

Atrophic subtype — induced by deficient trophic factors, nutrients, vitamins or hormonal imbalance, as in early hysterectomy, menopause, hypothyroidism, adrenal fatigue; some people have both inflammation and insulin resistance or diabetes, with a subtype called type 1.5 AD. Here the brain benefits from a low carb diet with flexibility to burn both ketones and glucose.

Cortical or toxic subtype — induced by environmental toxins in air/water, mycotoxins/mold, aflatoxins, wildfire smoke, heavy metals, pesticides, glyphosate (Round-Up), mercury fillings, tricholoroethylene, agent orange, Lyme disease, surgical implants and chronic inflammation. This form is new and different — a hidden epidemic showing up earlier in people in their 50's.

He has created a *personalized* therapeutic program (Bredesen Protocol™) to treat people with mild cognitive impairment and early Alzheimer's disease with demonstrable success. It's not one-size-fits-all — it's more like a roof with 36 holes, so plugging one hole is not enough.

This comprehensive, functional and lifestyle medicine program aims to optimize:

- **Nutrition** (low carb, healthy fat diet; avoid gluten, dairy, processed and fried foods)
- **Supplements** (various trophic vitamins, minerals, antioxidants, omega 3, etc.)
- **Fasting** (at least 12-16 hrs between dinner and next meal; fast 3 hrs before bedtime)
- **Exercise** (5-6 times per week for 30-60 min with cardio and strength training)
- **Sleep** (8 hrs a night; treat sleep apnea; use melatonin as needed)
- **Stress reduction** (music, meditation, yoga, pets, walk in the park)
- **Mental exercise** (crossword puzzles, Sudoku, learn a new language)
- **Auditory physiology** (binaural beat "meditation on steroids")
- **Hygiene** (oral, nasal, skin, nails, hair, gut)
- **Hormone therapy** (as needed for deficient sex hormones, thyroid, GH, etc.)

The program can be used by healthy people to *prevent* Alzheimer's disease and to optimize other areas of health at the same time, such as reversing obesity and diabetes, too. That means a longer life and a higher quality of life and less burden on society. It's a win-win-win!

What is the energetic basis of Alzheimer's disease? Most people think Alzheimer's or dementia is one of the worst things that can happen to us. Losing your mind, losing your bodily functions — what's worse than that? That may be true from the human perspective, but not necessarily from the soul's perspective.

The soul comes here to experience things in human form — the good, the bad and the ugly, too. It incarnates with a specific **life plan** that may include dealing with things like cancer, obesity, diabetes, stroke or Alzheimer's disease at some point in life. The soul arrives with specific **psycho-spiritual programming**, which sets up the conditions it wants to experience in human form. It may decide to fully experience and die from the condition. Or it may wish to overcome it in some way. All is choice. All is experience.

The soul has also pre-planned the timing and manner of **3-5 exit points** from this life (Chapter 15), which occur at different ages throughout life, according to Guy Needler ("The Anne Dialogues").

Alzheimer's disease and other forms of dementia are simply other ways to depart. Needler said in these conditions, the soul has chosen to leave the body in a gradual way. The day-to-day functionality starts to deteriorate. The person gets problems with memory, because the ego (personality) starts to move out of the body and the memories go with it (below).

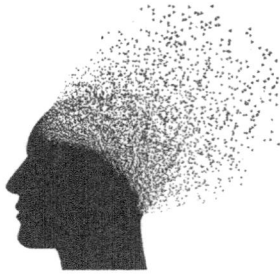

Note that when we die, the ego dissolves, but nothing is lost. That means we don't lose our unique personality traits, desires, quirks and all, because they are part of our energetic signature and experiential memory from this lifetime. Everything is being recorded by the soul's Higher Self in real time throughout life (see "Spiritual Guide To Our Afterlife").

Nevertheless, the person we knew is no longer there — we don't feel their personality or their spirit. We just see a physical body that may or may not choose to communicate with us. Susann Taylor Shier said it's almost like the person is getting used to "going to heaven" again, to forget what it's like here, because it has been so intense. They go out of body, then they come back — they go out and come back and go: "Oh, did I miss something?"

She suggests that the family and caretakers see it creatively. Love them and be with them while they are in those other spaces, even if it seems like they are not here with you. You can communicate with them on a *soul level*, even when they are out of body on the Other Side.

Give them permission to be there and say: "I know where you are and it's a beautiful place, and you have permission from me to be there." You are not going to say: "Oh my god, get back here in your body!" She said they are creating their own crossing over process. It's their process and they will leave when they are ready to do so.

What is happening at the soul level? Guy Needler ("Psycho-Spiritual Healing") explained that the *sentience* ("consciousness") of the soul does not sit in the brain, but in the *soul seat* (located in the chest behind the front aspect of the heart chakra). The brain is not the controlling reason for the cause of dementia, Alzheimer's disease or Parkinson's disease. Physiologically, it may appear that these conditions are a function of atrophy of the brain, but spiritually they are a function of the soul's desire to leave the incarnation in a gradual way.

Thus, people with dementia or Alzheimer's disease aren't all there, because their sentience is mostly gone. The person has probably finished their life plan and is feeling that there is no reason to be here. The soul wants to leave, but the person may feel a duty to stay for the family (i.e. those who are dependent on them for consolation, confidence, emotional reasons, below).

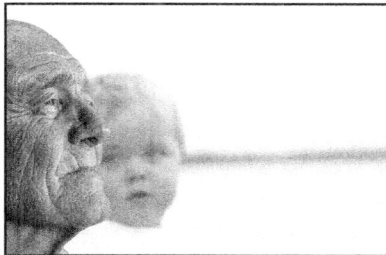

Those people who are around them all the time (e.g. spouse, caretaker) start to become part of the background, so the soul drifts out. When a new person (e.g. children, grandchildren) come to visit, it creates a focus for them, so part of their sentience comes back to the body to be there for them. They may be able to remember some things and talk about things for a while before they lose focus and start to drift out again. The visitors become part of the background, too (below).

The soul may think: "Oh well, they know I'm here now, so I can start to drift back." The soul can move back and forth, to and from the body, just like during gestation at the embryonic and fetal stages of life before the person was born.

We can give them permission to leave by telling them: "You can go back Home or back to your Higher Self. You don't need to hang around any longer." That will give them more incentive to fully detach from the human form, which will demise as soon as the sentient energies (that used to animate it) are removed from it (see "Spiritual Guide To Our Afterlife").

What happens in a coma? When someone lingers (e.g. coma), it's because they have a strong desire to stay incarnate and not let go of physicality. The ego is trying its hardest to stay incarnate, because it knows that the ego "disappears" when the human form demises. The ego's information is never lost and the soul always goes back to its Higher Self — no exceptions.

What's the point? There is a link between dementia and coma, because the sentience that usually animates the body and gives it a human personality isn't always there. In comatose people, the body is kept alive by a very small percentage of sentience and by medical and mechanical means. It is not animated or interactive with others — the eyes are generally closed in comatose people, while those with dementia have open eyes with a vacant look. Dementia is about the soul leaving the body, but not quite removing the connection totally.

Sometimes our souls want to get more "evolutionary brownie points" by experiencing life with and without certain abilities and functions (e.g. before dementia vs. after dementia, before stroke vs. after stroke). This allows other people to play the caretaker role, which may be challenging, but helps their soul evolve as well through service to others. Thus, as difficult as these situations may seem to be, many souls may benefit from them.

Some souls don't like to take the superfast roller coaster ride to the Other Side!

"Where you have been will start to feel farther removed, much like if you examined a past life experience. It will be easier to see the purpose of it all, and you will have little desire to drag any old energies with you, because you know they simply do not apply any longer. You will begin a fresh phase...This will feel very freeing for you!"— Shelley Young

CHAPTER 8

WHAT IS THE ENERGETIC BASIS OF DEPRESSION?

Now I'd like to explore what we know about Depression, since it is becoming more prevalent around the world, including more younger people than ever before.

What is the conventional view of depression? According to the World Health Organization (WHO), depression is the leading cause of disability worldwide affecting about 5% of the adult population. Over 300 million people of all ages suffer from this condition. Even though it is highly treatable, over 75% of people in poor countries receive no treatment, because of lack of resources and health care providers and the social stigma associated with mental disorders.

Depression is different from transient mood fluctuations that arise in response to our daily life challenges. There are many different types of depressive states that may vary in severity over time, including seasonal affective disorder. cyclothymia, bipolar disorder and major depression, which at worst may lead to suicide.

Persistent symptoms include feeling sad, irritable or empty, loss of pleasure or interest in activities, poor concentration, feelings of guilt, low self-worth, hopelessness, disrupted sleep, changes in appetite or weight, and feeling tired or low in energy. Children may manifest sadness, irritability, anger and acting out.

The cause of depression is unknown. It is thought to be a complex interaction of genetic, biological, social, environmental and psychological factors. People with depression have brain changes in certain parts that regulate mood, thinking, sleep, appetite and behavior. Generally, sadness, grief or depressive episodes may be triggered by **major life events** and negative or disruptive individual and collective experiences, such as:

• **Abuse** (physical abuse, sexual abuse, emotional abuse, torture, cyberbullying, etc.).

• **Age** (being elderly/young), lack of social support (being cast out from home/living alone)

• **Death or loss** of a loved one (partner/child/pet/ miscarriage)

• **Major life events** (graduation/retirement, new job/loss of job, getting married/divorced)

• **Substance abuse** (alcohol/drugs)

• **Chronic pain or incurable diseases** (heart, cancer, arthritis, thyroid)

• **Certain medications** (steroids, antiviral, acne drugs)

- **Global events** (e.g. pandemic, climate change, natural disasters, migrant crisis, threat of local/regional/world wars, authoritarianism, income and wealth inequality, social injustice, water/air/soil/airwave pollution, etc.)

There are many effective treatments for depression, including antidepressant medications and psychotherapy, which addresses the thinking and behavioral patterns that precipitate depression. There are several natural approaches that include targeting inflammation (e.g. gut microbiome) and stress by mindfulness meditation, daily exercise (endorphins), nutritional supplements (e.g. magnesium, B vitamins, curcumin, omega-3 fatty acids), dietary changes (e.g. keto diet, intermittent fasting), sunlight, acupuncture, social activity, etc. All of them help.

We are still in the midst of a viral pandemic and emergent "**climate grief**" or "**eco-anxiety**," as explained by Panu Pihkala in "Climate grief: How we mourn a changing planet?":

"For many middle-class citizens of industrialised nations this brings a profound existential challenge. The world is revealed to be much more tragic and fragile than people thought it was. For many young people, the climate crisis is the first enormous existential crisis that they face.

Climate grief comes in many forms. *There is the bereavement-like grief and trauma when a climate change-enhanced "natural disaster" hits you or your close ones… Then there is transitional grief: a growing awareness that things are changing, and feelings of grief and sadness because of the many losses involved…loss of human, animal and plant life, but also loss of identities, beliefs, and lifestyles." — Panu Pihkala (BBC Future)*

What is the energetic basis of depression? Are we doomed by all that is happening in our inner and outer worlds? That depends on us. These events are designed to help us remember our **connection** to each other, to nature and the planet as an interdependent web of life.

As sensitive, empathic sentient entities, whatever happens to one of us happens to all of us to some degree. We can feel it when the world is in turmoil around us (e.g. war). Those of us who are able to handle the changes will hold space for those who are struggling right now. We take turns in holding and handling things, as we continue to evolve together. How?

Each of us has a **life plan** with a unique **soul blueprint** or energetic design that tells us what we came to be and do in human form. It gives us clues as to which states of "beingness" we came here to explore (see "Spiritual Guide To Our Relationships"). Let's examine the archetypal functions of the Nine Types in a stepwise manner:

For example, there are at least **22 different "Gates of Melancholy"** described by Human Design, based on Ra Uru Hu's work ("The Complete Rave I'Ching"). If you have one of these gates in your blueprint, it doesn't mean you're doomed. Why?

Each gate can be expressed in three ways: The **Shadow** level corresponds to the ego's state of "melancholy." The **Gift** level shows what the soul wants to express, and the **Siddhi** level shows the most enlightened expression of the same gate. You get to explore all these states in human form, if you wish (see "Spiritual Guide To Our Relationships").

98

Here is a Table that summarizes the **22 Gates of Melancholy** (from various Human Design sources):

I CHING GATE Number & Name	MELANCHOLY PATTERN	SHADOW	GIFT	SIDDHI
1 Purpose	No one sees me as creative or fresh	Depression	Originality	Beauty
8 Contribution	No one is paying attention to me	Inauthenticity	Authenticity	Fulfillment
2 Direction	Feels lost, as things are moving too slowly	Disorientation	Orientation	Unity
14 Power Skills	Having to work to get power or recognition	Compromise	Competence	Prosperity
10 Self-Love	No one else knows how to behave	Self-Obsession	Naturalness	Being
20 The Now	Discomfort with the world as it is now	Superficiality	Self-Assurance	Presence
12 The Channel	There is no one worth telling anything to	Vanity	Discrimination	Purity
22 Openness	There is nothing worth listening to	Dishonor	Graciousness	Grace
25 Spirit of the Self	Feels insignificant, fears owning pain	Constriction	Acceptance	Unconditional Love
51 Shock	Lack of excitement or competition in life	Agitation	Initiative	Awakening
28 Risk taker	Life is devoid of purpose or challenge	Purposelessness	Tenacity	Immortality
38 Fighter	Struggling to know what to fight for	Stubbornness	Perseverance	Honor
39 Provocateur	Moody, not knowing whom to provoke	Provocation	Dynamism	Liberation
55 Faith in Spirit	Feels emptiness, lack, deflated spirit	Victimization	Freedom	Freedom
24 Rationalization	There is no inner silence in thought loops	Mental Anxiety	Invention	Silence
61 Mystery	Lack of inner inspiration, awe or wonder	Disenchantment	Inspiration	Inner Truth
23 Assimilation	Not being able to explain myself clearly	Complexity	Simplicity	Quintessence
43 Insight	No one hears me, they think I'm a freak	Deafness	Insight	Epiphany
3 Beginnings	Hard to begin, since nothing ever lasts	Chaos	Innovation	Innocence
60 Limitation	Hard to let go, I have nowhere to go	Limitation	Realism	Resourcefulness
34 Power	Angry, as not being able to use my power	Force	Outer Strength	Majesty
57 Intuition	Lack of self-trust, fear of the future	Unease	Intuition	Clarity

Note: All these gates are arranged in *specific pairs* that create **powerful energy channels** inside the body.

For example, Gate 1 (Purpose) is connected to Gate 8 (Contribution) to create the **Channel of the Creative Role Model.** Similarly, Gate 2 (Direction) links to Gate 14 (Power Skills) to create the **Channel of the Alchemist**, and so on. These channels connect specific chakras or energy centers to move energy around the body (see Chapter 2).

When we are depressed, we feel low in energy, because our energy is not moving around properly. As Anodea Judith ("Eastern Body, Western Mind") noted, depression is basically a state of *undercharge* or a lack of excitement or enthusiasm in our chakras.

The chakras become undercharged, when energy is held back or "blocked" by something, such as fear (at root chakra), guilt (sacral chakra), shame (solar chakra), grief (heart chakra), deceit (throat chakra), illusion (third eye chakra), or attachment (crown chakra).

Each chakra has its own characteristic **manifestations** of deficiency of energy, according to Judith (below):

Chakras	Deficiency of Energy
	Apathy, spiritual cynicism, rigid belief systems, learning difficulties
	Denial, insensitive, lack of imagination Difficulty seeing the future
	Fear of speaking, weak voice, shy Can't put feelings into words
	Depressed, antisocial, withdrawn Lonely, cold hearted, narcissist
	Low energy, weak will, cold, passive Victim mentality, low self-esteem
	Lack of desire, passion or excitement Denial of pleasure, rigidity, fear of sex
	Disconnected from body, poor focus Poor finances, restless, anxious

Root chakra deficiency: disconnected from the body, poor focus, poor discipline, poor boundaries, poor finances, fearful, anxious, restless, can't settle, often disorganized.

Sacral chakra deficiency: lack of desire, passion or excitement, denial of pleasure or joy, excessive boundaries, rigidity, poor social skills, fear of sex, fear of change, etc.

Solar chakra deficiency: low energy, weak will, low self-esteem, easily manipulated, victim mentality, passive, cold physically, poor follow through, unreliable, poor digestion, etc.

Heart chakra deficiency: depressed, lonely, withdrawn, antisocial, cold hearted, fear of intimacy, fear of relationships, intolerant of self or others, lack of empathy, narcissist, etc.

Throat chakra deficiency: introverted, shy, weak voice, fear of speaking, fear of persecution, difficulty putting feelings into words, tone deaf, poor sense of timing or rhythm, etc.

Third eye chakra deficiency: poor vision, poor memory, poor dream recall, denial (can't see what's going on), insensitive, polarized to one side, poor visualization, lack of imagination, etc.

Crown chakra deficiency: apathy, learning difficulties, rigid belief systems, spiritual cynicism, excess in lower chakras (e.g. materialism, greed, domination of others), etc.

How do we heal the chakra deficiencies? First, determine which chakra(s) are the most affected by energy deficiency. Also check the character structures (Chapter 3) that show how energy flows through the body. Then reclaim the body in energetic terms by customizing the healing practices for any affected chakras, as suggested by Anodea Judith:

Root chakra deficiency: reconnect with body using some physical activity, aerobics, hiking, dancing, weight lifting, touch, massage, yoga, grounding, psychotherapy for safety and security.

Sacral chakra deficiency: movement therapy, emotional release, inner child work, develop healthy boundaries, self-nurturing and pleasuring practices, 12-step programs (for addiction), etc.

Solar chakra deficiency: risk taking, grounding practices, stress control, martial arts, vigorous exercise, calisthenics, psychotherapy for anger, shame, will, autonomy issues, etc.

Heart chakra deficiency: breathing exercises, journaling, inner child work, psychotherapy for grief feeling and release, forgiveness, codependency, self-acceptance, self-love issues, etc.

Throat chakra deficiency: singing, chanting, toning, storytelling, automatic and creative writing, psychotherapy for communication skills, inner child work, fear of persecution, etc.

Third eye chakra deficiency: creating visual artwork, guided visualizations, meditation, psychotherapy for dream work, memory work, past life regression, hypnosis, etc.

Crown chakra deficiency: reestablish spirit connection, spiritual discipline, meditation, psychotherapy for working on belief systems, inner observer, connecting to Higher Self, etc.

What's the point? I hope this helps you see Depression as a complicated condition with many layers and levels of understanding. Some people have proposed a new way to think about depression. They see it as an existential shift in how the person experiences life — a distinct state of consciousness, like waking, dreaming, and drug induced states. All these states have different capacities to think, feel, and interact with the world. This helps to explain the ebb and flow of the depressive symptoms over time.

This way of thinking is not too far off, when you consider that depression results from the **shadow level** of existence, which is a valid experience, just like any other frequency we choose to explore in life. We have experiences, but we are not that experience. Think of it like pain linked to an underlying problem that requires treatment — the pain itself needs treatment, as noted by Mark D. White, PhD ("Is Depression Actually a Unique State of Consciousness?").

In the *old spiritual paradigm*, we are used to growing through **suffering**, whereas in the *new spiritual paradigm*, we are growing through **healing**. We have to heal the body, the head and the heart, as suggested by Anodea Judith and others to strengthen our central channel that connects us to "Heaven" (Gate 1 of Purpose) and grounds us to "Earth" (Gate 2 of Direction). That's how we can become walking vortices of sentient energy while embodied in the human form.

Wendy Kennedy said that depression is lack of connection or **perceived disconnection from Source energy**. You are never separate from Source/God, but you are cutting off Source energy to a trickle when you are depressed. What you need to do is come back to the **heart center** (soul seat), where you are present and grounded.

That's easier said than done when you are in a dark or difficult space, but she suggested you make a list of all the things that uplift you (e.g. certain music, a spot in nature, a friend that makes you laugh, a movie you like to watch, etc.) — anything that opens your heart or makes you laugh, feel lighter or more carefree.

According to Kennedy, **breath is the great connector**, because it moves energy at both the physical level and energetic field level. When you are breathing consciously, you are moving more energy and reinforcing your conscious awareness of your connection to Source.

The other thing is to take the focus off yourself and your limiting programs and beliefs. The fastest way to do that is to **find some way to be of service** — volunteer your time, help your friends, do something for someone else. That will help you get into that *heart centered* space faster, where your **Soul Self** is waiting for you to listen to its guidance going forward (below).

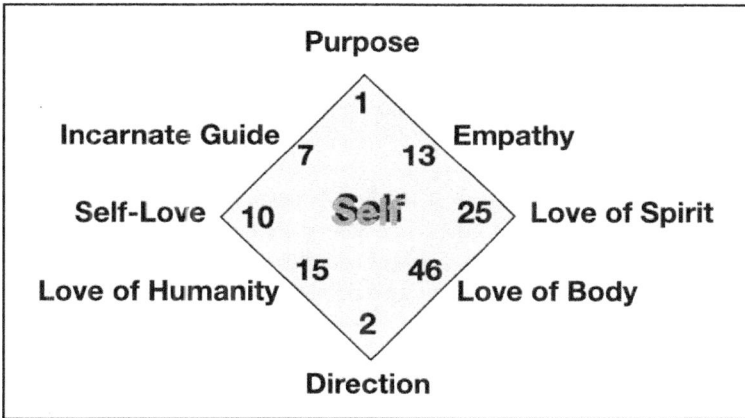

"Our sorrows and wounds are healed only when we touch them with compassion." — *Gautama Buddha*

CHAPTER 9

WHAT IS THE ENERGETIC BASIS OF ADDICTION?

What is the conventional view of addiction? The term **"addiction"** refers to the condition of being addicted to a particular substance, thing, or activity. There are several types of addictions that include substances, thoughts, feelings, people and activities, some of which are shown in "The Addiction Tree" along with some underlying traumas or issues found in unhealthy or **dysfunctional families** that most of us are born into (below).

What is the cause of addiction? Several models have been postulated for why some people become addicted and others don't. Here is a brief summary of the models used over the years:

• **Moral model** of past centuries viewed addiction as a character flaw and a sin, which justified punishing addicts with beatings, fines, jail or public humiliation.

• **Disease model** suggests that addiction is a chronic relapsing disease that is progressive unless treated by lifelong abstinence (Alcoholics Anonymous model).

• **Psycho-dynamic model** maintains that we can link our problems to our childhood, which affects how we cope or don't cope as adults (psychotherapy or counseling model).

• **Social learning model** sees substance dependence as not only chemical but also behavioral and social in nature, based on thoughts about the substance and being under the influence of it.

• **Socio-cultural model** focuses on society as a whole. Drug use is linked to culturally and socially disadvantaged people, whose environment needs to be changed (e.g. poverty, housing).

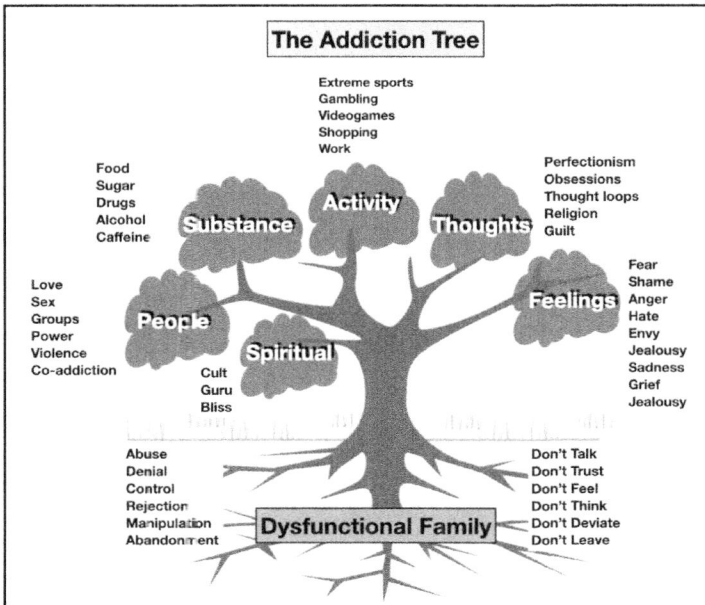

The Addiction Tree

Extreme sports
Gambling
Videogames
Shopping
Work

Food
Sugar
Drugs
Alcohol
Caffeine

Substance

Activity

Perfectionism
Obsessions
Thought loops
Religion
Guilt

Thoughts

Love
Sex
Groups
Power
Violence
Co-addiction

People

Feelings

Fear
Shame
Anger
Hate
Envy
Jealousy
Sadness
Grief
Jealousy

Spiritual

Cult
Guru
Bliss

Abuse
Denial
Control
Rejection
Manipulation
Abandonment

Dysfunctional Family

Don't Talk
Don't Trust
Don't Feel
Don't Think
Don't Deviate
Don't Leave

What is the effect of addiction in families? John Bradshaw ("The Family: A Revolutionary Way of Self-Discovery") said that 96% of all families are to some degree emotionally impaired or dysfunctional. The rules handed down from one generation to another are unhealthy and make our families and societies sick. Why?

Our consciousness and way of life have radically changed in the last 150 years, but our parenting rules haven't. They're out of date and toxic, because they're based on obedience, orderliness, cleanliness and control of emotions and desires. They're authoritarian and use shame-based programming to control and enslave the soul of the child, to dim their light and keep them from accessing their own power.

A dysfunctional family is one with multiple internal and external influences.

The *internal* influences include parent-child conflicts, sibling rivalries, domestic violence, mental illness, etc.

The *external* factors may involve drug or alcohol abuse, gambling, extramarital affairs, physical illness, unemployment, etc. These negative influences affect the basic needs of every family member. To cope, they develop rigid **family roles** that are not chosen or flexible (below). Each individual exists to keep the dysfunctional family system in balance, but in the process they all become **co-dependent**, living in *reaction* to the family distress.

For example, if Dad is a workaholic, one of the children becomes Mom's Surrogate Spouse. If Dad is an alcoholic, one child will be a Hero, because the family needs some dignity. The Scapegoat is the troublemaker, who acts out the family's unexpressed anger and pain. The Forgotten Child is the quiet one, who carries the loneliness and isolation of the marriage. The Clown uses humor or mischief to break the tension and lighten everyone's load, and so on.

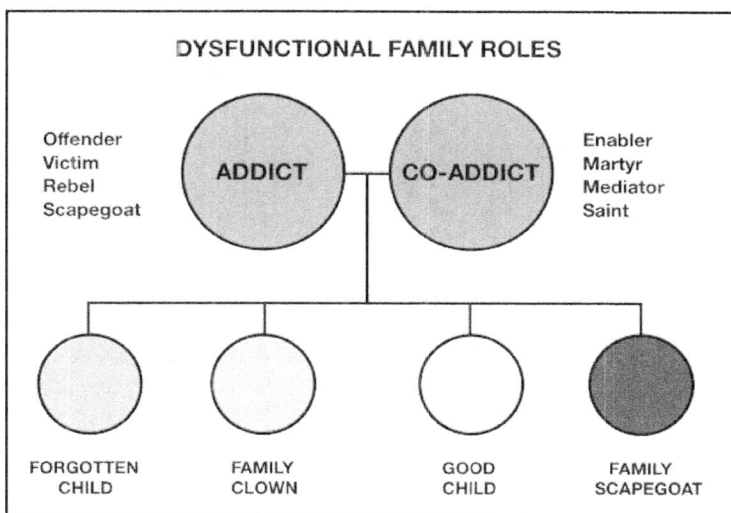

When dysfunctional people marry other dysfunctional people, they create new dysfunctional families or a **multigenerational pattern,** which is difficult to break, according to Bradshaw.

Note that each child may play **multiple roles** in a dysfunctional family with respect to mom and dad's preferences or dislikes, including the surrogate spouse, confidante, little princess, dad's buddy, parent's parent, caretaker, family counselor/referee, sick one with physical illness, religious one, pretty/cute one, genius/overachiever, peacemaker, loser, rascal, the problem, etc.

When these trauma patterns are intergenerational in origin, they are passed on from the grandparents to the parents to their children. There is no getting away from trauma — it affects all of us one way or another, when we lose our sense of self, connection or value in the world.

Here are examples of **intergenerational trauma patterns** in survivors across the world (below):

Surviving Wars	Surviving Slavery	Surviving Colonialism
Post-Traumatic Stress Syndrome	Post-Traumatic Slave Syndrome	Post-Traumatic Oppression Syndrome
Racial Violence	Dehumanization	Culture / Identity Loss
Domestic Violence	Internalized Racism	Social Caste Hierarchy
Sexual Abuse	Sexual Abuse	Sexual Abuse
Drug / Alcohol Abuse	Domestic Violence	Ethnic Violence
Emotional Repression	Vacant Self-Esteem	Poverty Consciousness
Memory Gaps	Depression	Shame-based Rules
Chronic Pain	Hopelessness	Self-hatred
Sleep Problems	Abandonment	Severe Anxiety
Shame / Guilt	Hypervigilance	Depression

These trauma patterns also affect the **attachment styles** between children and their caretakers, which in turn affect their intimate, social and work relationships as adults. They also mold our physical health, epigenetics, boundaries in families and friendships, and even our political and religious views, interactions with authority figures, societal systems and more (see "Spiritual Guide To Our Awakening").

There is no "one-size-fits-all" healing method, but there are many **trauma healing** modalities, as described by Lissa Rankin, MD ("What Actually Heals Trauma?") that include energy healing tools, spiritual reSourcing, psycho-spiritual healing, psycho-education, understanding adaptive survival strategies, treating negative core beliefs, embodied meditation practices, learning to regulate the nervous system, somatic therapies, expressive arts therapy, mindful self-compassion, faith-based programs, rewriting your story, and more.

What is the energetic basis of addiction? We can look at addictions from the human perspective, but it's often helpful to see them from the soul's perspective. Remember the *soul* is the driver and the human body is the *vehicle* for incarnation, which exists at ten frequency levels and has seven major chakras (Chapter 2).

The traumas and abuses affect certain chakras more than others. For example, physical abuse, violence, abandonment and survival issues (e.g. holocaust, poverty, famine, migration) affect primarily the *first chakra*, while sexual abuse, neglect, coldness, rejection, manipulation, enmeshment, emotional repression and alcoholic families traumatize the *second chakra*.

Third chakra abuses include physical abuse, shaming, authoritarianism or domination of will, while *fourth chakra* issues include betrayal, divorce, death of a loved one, grief, a loveless or conditional love environment. *Fifth chakra* traumas may arise from verbal abuse, lies, mixed messages, secrets, constant yelling, fear of persecution by authoritarian or alcoholic parents.

Sixth chakra issues arise from frightening environments (e.g. war zones, violent scenes), denial of reality and invalidation of intuition ("sixth sense"). *Seventh chakra* abuses include misinformation, forced religiosity or blind obedience to any belief system, spiritual abuse, bypassing or addiction, as observed by Anodea Judith ("Eastern Body, Western Mind").

According to Anodea Judith, **addictions** are difficult to classify in terms of chakras, because different substances produce **different states** (seen as overexpression or underexpression). But each chakra also represents a specific **developmental stage**. They evolve in sequence from the bottom up with our chronological age — from the root (0-1 yr) to sacral (2 yrs) to solar (4 yrs) to heart (7 yrs) to throat (12 yrs) to third eye (adolescence) to crown chakra (adulthood).

Here is a Figure that lists some of the **common addictions** to show which ones are related to specific chakras and their issues (based on Anodea Judith's work).

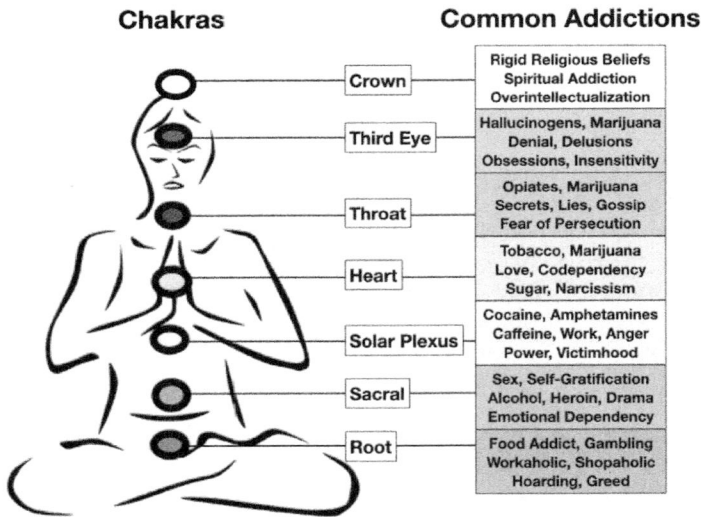

Chakras   **Common Addictions**

Chakra	Common Addictions
Crown	Rigid Religious Beliefs, Spiritual Addiction, Overintellectualization
Third Eye	Hallucinogens, Marijuana, Denial, Delusions, Obsessions, Insensitivity
Throat	Opiates, Marijuana, Secrets, Lies, Gossip, Fear of Persecution
Heart	Tobacco, Marijuana, Love, Codependency, Sugar, Narcissism
Solar Plexus	Cocaine, Amphetamines, Caffeine, Work, Anger, Power, Victimhood
Sacral	Sex, Self-Gratification, Alcohol, Heroin, Drama, Emotional Dependency
Root	Food Addict, Gambling, Workaholic, Shopaholic, Hoarding, Greed

The way we cope with stress and trauma at the chakra level may be manifest as increasing energy to *fight* the stress (seen as lashing out or overexpression of anger with emotional, verbal or physical reactivity) or as decreasing energy to *withdraw* from it (seen as shutting down with fear, underexpression or repression of self). This is a **coping mechanism** that explains why we might want to *stimulate* or *depress* the energies at certain chakras in certain situations.

By the way, **choosing the body** is one of the most important choices the **soul** makes before incarnation. The soul knows that the human form is the most complicated and most addictive form in the universe. Why? Because we exist at the bottom of the multiverse.

The lower the frequency we exist at, the greater the chance of losing our higher frequency thoughts, behaviors, actions and higher functions (e.g. telepathic and empathic communication). On Earth, we lose about 99% of our connectivity with our Higher Self. That means it's much easier to become addicted, attracted or attached to "**karma**" or lower frequency thoughts, behaviors, actions, sensory stimuli and experiences. But our souls agree to do it anyway, according to Guy Needler ("Avoiding Karma"). Why?

Why would souls choose addiction? Needler said we do it to **give ourselves choice**. Only brave souls agree to come to Earth, the densest and hardest place to exist in. It's like a graduate school for incarnation. The souls understand what they're getting into and know the limitations of the environment and do it willingly. Why?

We agree to be here, because the **evolutionary opportunities** for our souls and Higher Selves far outweigh the difficulties and isolation/separation we encounter briefly while incarnate. Even if we make a "mistake" or take a wrong turn, we still progress just by being here, because it is so profoundly different from our energetic existence.

Some souls are born into a family setting to experience some level of addiction, because they want to experience what it's like to come out of the addiction. Others in that family may show the way (or not). Some souls become addicted, and it may take them dozens or thousands of lifetimes to come out of it. It's like a bad habit or a familiar pattern that they fall into, according to Gordon Phinn ("You Are History"). But that's also part of the game of incarnation.

Needler said the whole objective of being here is to **become self-aware and detach ourselves from these addictions**, so we can navigate through the incarnation without accruing karma. Often what seems like "minor evolution" for our soul becomes "major evolution" for our Higher Self, when we detach from karmic attachments. We all benefit from it in the end (see "Spiritual Guide To Our Multiverse").

How many addictions are there? David R. Hawkins said that there are over 650 addictions. But Needler said it's probably limitless. There are as many types of addictions as we can think of in terms of the ways we can interact with ourselves, with each other, our environment and the things we create in our environment.

For example, the new virtual and augmented reality technologies ("metaverse") are just other ways to become addicted to the physical plane (below). Some types of addictions (e.g. video games, extreme sports) didn't even exist in earlier lifetimes.

There are variations upon variations upon variations. The whole point of us being here is to experience things first-hand, to be in the thick of it all, to be the actor in the movie, not just the couch potato watching the movie.

But we are also meant to learn as we go, and to overcome all physical addictions in order to master incarnation at some point in our soul's evolution within the physical universe (see "Spiritual Guide To Our Awakening").

What is the best way to overcome addictions? Needler said anything that allows you to detach yourself from certain thoughts, behaviors and actions and sensory stimuli is a positive way of overcoming addictions. What works for you might not work for somebody else, but a variation of it might work. Here are a few things to consider:

Therapy, counseling, rehab, lifestyle modification, diet changes, fasting, turning off the news, prayer, meditation, contemplation, disconnecting from electronics, being in nature are various ways to "reset" yourself. Self-analysis and using the observer self are other ways. The 12 step program is another way, as is becoming a hermit or a yogi that detaches himself from interacting with others, as happened more often in the past.

Some people like support groups, others like alone time to process issues. The way that works for YOU is the best way, as long as it's repeatable, robust and effective for you.

You will know that you are protected from addictions or karma, when you can do things (e.g. eat chocolate, smoke marijuana, go on a roller coaster ride, watch a movie, have two or three cars, etc.), but you don't get attached to those things. You won't have an overwhelming desire to experience that thing again and again. That way you don't get the links to it or attached to something that is potentially addictive and holds you down (like sandbags tied to your feet).

You may choose to experience it, work with it, learn from it and then choose to move away from it. You may choose to change the way you operate, think, behave and act as a result of it, which is part of your evolutionary progression.

What's the point? Looking at the Addiction Tree, it's clear that ALL of us in human form are prone to addictions of one kind or another, whether it's chocolate, shopping, sex, drugs, power or attention. We're trying to get that lift or "hit" from something external to us. We want a quick fix, as noted by Wendy Kennedy ("The Great Human Potential").

She said the addiction is created, because **you're not connecting with Source** or God energy. If we really want to **heal addiction**, it's about creating a deeper connection within yourself to Source by raising your own frequency. That's how you rise above the addictive frequencies.

The other problem is that if we keep telling ourselves the **same story** of who we think we are, we're never going to change. At some point, you have to stop telling yourself that you are an **"addict,"** because that will keep you in a loop with that story at a particular frequency range. You have to let go of that story of who you think you are (e.g. addict, good girl, troublemaker, etc.) and any limiting beliefs about what you're capable of. Throw those old, worn out "costumes" away and say this instead:

"I acknowledge and express my divine authority in each moment." – Wendy Kennedy

You are free to heal now. You are free to release all self-imposed limitations, because you don't have to stick to a particular story. The same thing goes for any conscious or unconscious familial, ancestral, collective human or even "star seed" stories that hold us back with health issues, poverty consciousness, curses/dark magic, limiting beliefs, worries, war stories, etc.

You can observe your overall behavior, and one day you'll let go of the "label" and keep working on your inner connection to Source/God, which is who you really are. You are an individualized unit of Source sent to *experience* things on its behalf to increase its sentience (consciousness). **That means you're not a flawed, broken, sinful or unworthy person.** Neither were your parents or the "bad others" we tend to blame for the problems in our life, as noted by John Welwood ("Perfect Love, Imperfect Relationships").

Nora Herold suggested that we **see alcohol for what it is** — *a tool for enslavement* used on this planet for eons. Get out of judgment, guilt and shame about addiction. The enslavement game is over now. You don't need to play that game any longer in human form. Get into loving yourself more as a being with your own sovereignty and agency. You are Love incarnate, as is everybody else. You're never NOT having a spiritual moment in life, according to Herold.

Needler said we are *creator entities in training* to become Source Entities in our own right in the far distant future. Let that sink in for a moment! We have many things to learn along the way, but we can ask for help from our Higher Self, guide and helpers and all the people around us, because we're all in this together.

Herold said when you find yourself feeling powerless, defeated, abandoned or feeling shame, anger, sadness, grief or your darkness, feel it, own it and take responsibility for it. The reason you gave it to yourself is because **you want to heal and transmute it**, not just the trauma from your childhood but from other lifetimes on the Earth and elsewhere. It's just a hook, a memory, but you're off the hook now, you don't have to be an addict any longer.

"Remind yourself you can't screw this up! Operate from JOY." – Nora Herold

Here is a healing technic given by Herold to help you transmute trauma in the moment, as it happens. It just takes a couple of minutes to do the **FOAL** (Feel-Observe-Accept-Love) method:

FEEL — simply feel what you're feeling and own it (using "I" statements): Ah, I'm feeling sad, I'm feeling anxious, I'm feeling angry, I'm feeling pain in my knee, etc. Feel what you must, don't push it away.

OBSERVE — while you're fully feeling, begin to observe yourself from a balcony, while you're still feeling the intensity of your experience without judgment. Then you've got the 3D self feeling away, and your 5D consciousness observing, which gives you a blended 3D/5D experience.

ACCEPT — step into acceptance saying: I totally, completely accept myself and this feeling state in this moment exactly as I am.

LOVE — what happens next is an automatic activation of **unconditional love** within your energetic system that gets sent to all versions of you that have felt that trauma — wherever it sits, on whatever timeline it sits, and whatever moment in this lifetime and any other lifetime you experienced that trauma going back to the origin of that trauma. You will feel lighter right away.

Smile! When things get intense and you get triggered by something external to you, just FOAL more often. **Be more gentle, loving and compassionate with yourself** during this highly polarized time on Earth. Keep doing your inner work.

When you clear something at the energetic level, you don't need to play it out in your physical reality brought to your attention as pain or dis-ease in your physical body or as turbulence in your environment. Feel-Observe-Accept-Love. Rinse and repeat.

"You cannot have a fair assessment of yourselves if you are only looking for what you consider to be wrong with you or requiring fixing — stop making yourself the villain in your story and consider that you just might be the hero."
— *Shelley Young*

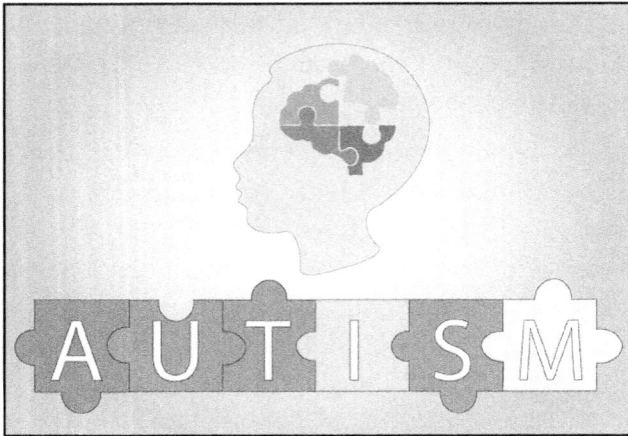

CHAPTER 10

WHAT IS THE ENERGETIC BASIS OF AUTISM?

Now I'd like to describe a few poorly understood mental conditions that are becoming more prevalent in our younger people, who are born with a different energetic blueprint than their predecessors. One such condition is what we call "Autism."

What is the conventional view of autism? Autism spectrum disorder (ASD) is considered a developmental disability, because people with ASD may communicate, interact, behave, and learn in ways that are different from other people, as noted from babyhood onwards (below).

According to the Centers for Disease Control (CDC), ASD occurs in all racial, ethnic and socioeconomic groups. It is more common among boys (1 in 42) than in girls (1 in 189) with an average prevalence of about 1-2.6% worldwide. ASD now includes several conditions that used to be diagnosed separately: autistic disorder, pervasive developmental disorder not otherwise specified (PDD-NOS), and Asperger syndrome or so-called "high-functioning" autism.

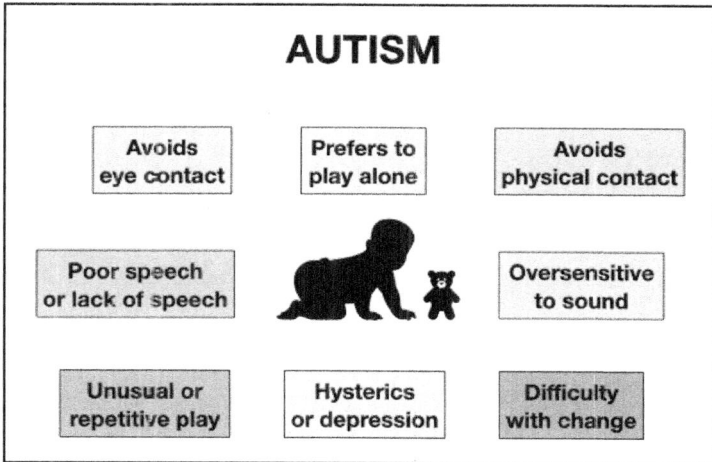

The cause of ASD is unknown, but is related to genetic, biologic and environmental factors (e.g. certain drugs taken during pregnancy, older parents, toxins, vaccines, etc.). More people are being diagnosed with ASD, which is based solely on the child's development and characteristic behavior patterns. There is no cure for ASD. Its prevalence seems to be increasing at a rate that is alarming to some people.

The learning, thinking, and problem-solving abilities of people with ASD can range from gifted to severely challenged. Some people with ASD need a lot of help in their daily lives, while others need less help, as depicted in the popular movies *Rain Man* (1988), *Temple Grandin* (2010) and others. Grandin said she has succeeded *because* she has autism. She said: "I'm different, not less." She's right about that!

What is the energetic basis of autism? Guy Needler ("Psycho-Spiritual Healing") is the first person to give us a newer understanding of autism from the *soul's perspective.* The energetic view of ASD is totally different. This condition can result from several different situations, which explain the variations in the spectrum. Let's go through them one by one.

Soul's life plan: Basically, it is how the soul has *chosen* to incarnate — it is part of the soul's life plan, so it can have a different life experience in human form. The **parents** have no part or influence whatsoever on the energetic state of their offspring. The child's soul organized this condition prior to inserting itself into a particular human body. Therefore, the parents need to release any fears, worries, guilt, shame, remorse, anger or sense of karmic burden regarding the child — the child chose you to be its parent for a good reason.

Type of energy set: In the womb, the soul inserts an **energy system** into the zygote as an interface with the physical body, so the soul can animate it. Think of the body as a "car" and the soul as the "driver." The soul can come in and out of the body at will and does that regularly throughout the pregnancy and even after birth. But in autistics, the energy system is special, because it allows the soul to connect to higher frequencies than most people around them. Why?

To answer that, we need to review how humanity is evolving. Dolores Cannon ("The Three Waves of Volunteers") described the souls, who have been coming to Earth since the middle 1940's onwards. They came here to bring us out of the "dark ages" or low frequencies after all the World Wars. They arrived as the first, second or third

waves of volunteers or **way-showers**, who did a lot of inner work on their shadows to increase their own frequencies, which influenced their local areas and others on the globe as well (below).

For this reason, the **newer generations** are now able to incarnate as higher frequency versions of humans that we call the *indigo*, *crystal* and *rainbow children* or various combinations of these types, such as the indigo-crystal, indigo-rainbow, crystal-rainbow or hybrids of all three (below).

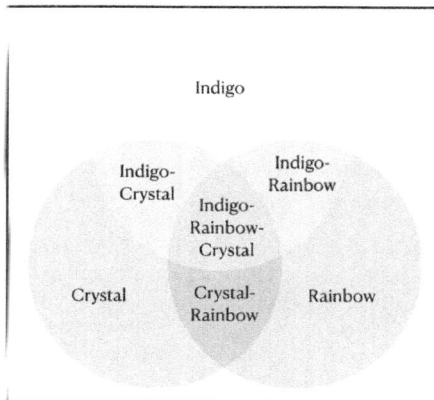

They are souls like us, but they incarnate into a slightly *modified* human form (below). Their body looks the same, but has a new higher frequency "**energy set**" that allows them to have a different life experience (see "Spiritual Guide To Our Awakening").

People with ASD have a half-hybrid energy set — meaning autistics have one half of a rainbow energy set, or one half of the crystal energy set, or one half of the indigo energy set. That makes them half-indigo, half-crystal or half-rainbow. The other half is the standard human energy set that most people have. That makes their life experience different.

Connectivity to higher frequencies: Autistics are *semi-connected* all the time to one-half of those higher frequency energy sets. They don't know how they do it, but they have a way of unlocking higher communication with their Higher Self. Think of it as a supernormal radio (below, right) that can access up to ten stations with ultra-high or mega-high frequencies compared to a standard human radio that can tune into just three stations (below, left).

Autistics have more connectivity and they are connected all the time. That can give them **sensory overload**, because they experience everything holistically or all at once. Most of us have barriers or filters around ourselves and each other from birth to death. In the process, we're missing out on the empathic, telepathic and many other types of communication mediums that are part of a higher frequency being, according to Needler (below).

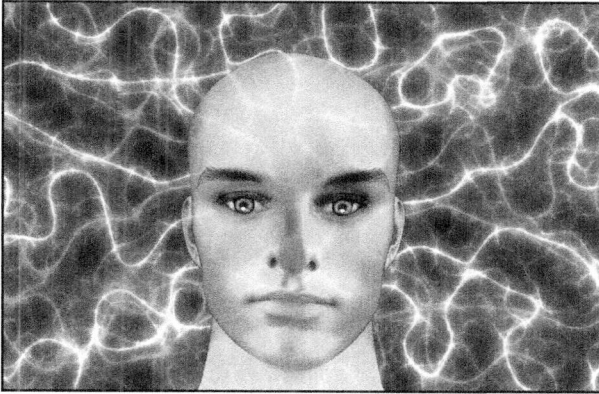

The level of autism depends on the person's connectivity to higher frequencies. A highly functional person has access to all ten levels (e.g. savant, genius), while a less functional person (who needs help with daily functions) can access a little more than the standard or "neurotypical" human. Those with medium connectivity are somewhere in between the two extremes.

These **higher intuitive functions** make autistics more like "supernormal" or "future" humans. The way they work is right for them. They just need to trust the connection they have and not try to conform to how they are told to work by standard humans at home, school or work.

For example, if they have *telepathic communication*, they don't need to talk much. If they have *empathic communication*, they don't need to hug somebody to know what's in their heart. If they have *intuitive intelligence*, they don't need to do math the hard way by solving equations and such, because they know the answer. They get it from their "superconsciousness" or the greater reality (Chapter 3).

All these things mean that they represent an advanced human being, who have a higher operating system than most of us. Their ability, thought processes and functions may be associated with the **fifth level** (FB 5), but they may close down, because their **physical form** is in the **third level** (FB 1-3), where the rest of us operate. For example, they may categorize things or sort things out in a very structured way, log them down and put them in a matrix, because that's the only way they can interface with us or try to understand how we operate. They themselves see things in a more holistic way.

They are designed for **communal connectivity** with others like them. Sometimes they incarnate here expecting to be in a reality where others like them can communicate, share and work together. But most of us aren't like that at all, so they get frustrated with us. It's like we are speaking a different language — we don't get them and they don't get us. It's as if they are in the wrong place at the wrong time, because there aren't too many people like them here (only 2% or so worldwide).

Chakra system: Here is another difference seen in ASD. If they are functioning on higher chakra levels, meaning the heart, throat, third eye and crown chakras, they don't need to be so anchored to their lower chakras. The lower three chakras (root, sacral, and solar plexus) combine to form one bigger **composite chakra** that animates and supports their physical body, which is not such a heavy anchor for them (below). This changes the way they *experience* their physical body or lower chakra functions.

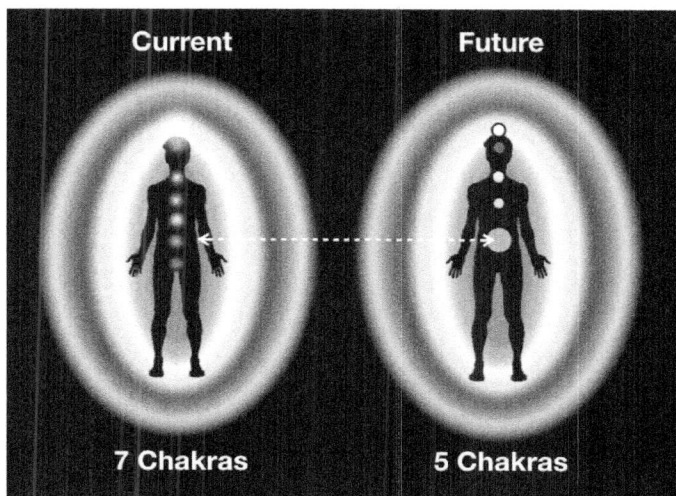

When we look at the **energetic blueprints** of people on the Autism-Asperger spectrum, we can map certain thoughts, behaviors and actions to specific **chakras** and **functions** (below). They share some common features, but each person has a unique combination of gates and traits.

Their gates and channels in the **upper chakras** may give them a higher level of *perception* and *metacognition* (below). This gives them a different life experience from most people around them in terms of being able to understand advanced logical and abstract concepts, getting new insights, instant knowing or higher intuitive functions (listed in Chapter 2) and a holistic view of life with more imagination, out of body experiences, creativity, etc. This is "normal" for them.

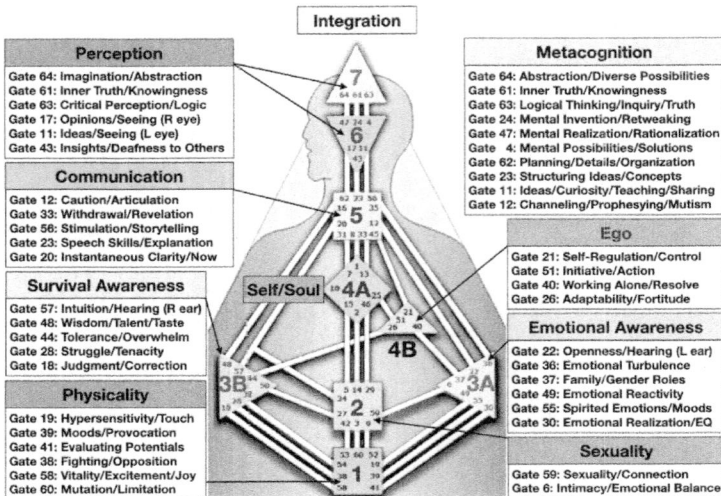

But their process is different from others, so they need to work with these functions in their own way, instead of trying to suppress or shut them down, as happens with *depression* (see Chapter 8) or *mental anxiety* (e.g. fear of mental loops/no silence in the mind, fear of speaking out/ not being able to express yourself clearly, fear of being seen as a freak vs. a genius, fear of being persecuted/ ostracized, fear of having no one to tell anything to/no one to listen to, etc.).

They can have *hyperesthesia* that affects one or more of their senses. Some are supersensitive to *sounds* via Gate 57 of Intuitive Hearing/Clairvoyance or Gate 22 of Openness to Listening/Not (e.g. speaking out of turn or improperly emoting, which pushes people away).

Some may be sensitive to *visual stimuli* via Gate 11 of Ideas/Light (with fear of darkness) or Gate 17 of Opinions/ Farsightedness (with fear of challenge to your opinions) or have extra sensitivity to certain *tastes* via Gate 48 of

Intuitive Taste or *smells* via Gate 44 of Alertness/Intuitive Smell (as shown above). They can also have *synesthesia*, where they experience one sense through another sense (e.g. hearing music and seeing colors in your mind).

Their **lower chakras** work differently as well. Since the **composite chakra** takes over the physical functions in the first three chakras, it may affect the expression of their *physicality*, *sexuality* and *emotional awareness* as a result. This gives them a different life experience as well.

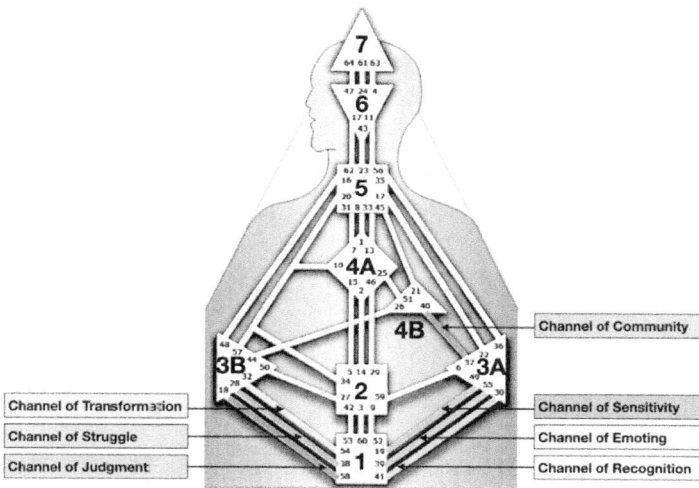

For example, many of them are **supersensitive** to *touch*, textures or physical contact, because they have Gate 19 of Touch/Attunement (root chakra, labeled as "1" in the above figure) that can lead to isolation and/or Gate 49 of Emotional Reactivity (solar plexus chakra/3A) that can range from being inert to reactive or rejecting. These two gates create the **Channel of Sensitivity** between the root and solar plexus (above). Autism is rooted in this channel, according to Karen Curry ("Understanding Human Design") and others, but there is much more to consider.

They can get easily **overwhelmed** by too many conversations (e.g. party), too much stress (e.g. school), too many changes (e.g. traveling, changing routines), and emotional outbursts (e.g. people fighting). Many autistics have the **Channel of Emoting** between Gate 39 of Provocateur/Moodiness (root), which feels or provokes tension around them, but may get overwhelmed and panics with the lack, emptiness or victimhood felt in Gate 55 of Faith/Abundance (solar plexus).

Many autistics have the **Channel of Recognition of Feelings** between Gate 30 of Desires/Clinging Fire/ Intensity (solar plexus) and Gate 41 of Anticipation/Fantasy (root) that can make them dreamy or hyperactive for a new experience, which may feel too intense (like burning fire), overwhelming and cause *burnout*. There is *emotional anxiety* about what might or might not happen. Their half-human/half-hybrid energy set may leave them with a "half-lived" experience. Most humans feel their way through life, but autistics may not recognize their feelings fully.

They need **alone time** — many have one or more of the "**gates of aloneness**" that include Gate 12 of Caution/ Articulation/Mutism, Gate 33 of Withdrawal/Retreat/ Privacy, and Gate 40 of Aloneness/Exhaustion/Restoration to rest and recharge. They need a "sensory free bubble" or retreat with some dim lights, quiet space or noise cancelling headphones, soft pillows and blankets using Gate 56 of Stimulation/Distraction by furry pets, soothing music, pretty lights, soft clothes or activities with repetitive movements (e.g. rocking back/forth, pacing, dancing), as suggested by the Instagram artist @autism_sketches (which is an excellent resource for autistic people, their friends, family and teachers).

The "**stimming**" helps them release **root chakra pressure**, bursts of energy or electric currents flowing through them, so they can reconnect to their body to feel safe and grounded. This is how they can manage *sensory overload* and calm down in a safe space, which is a basic necessity (just like sleeping) for their well-being to prevent *autistic fatigue* and *burnout*, which is related to all aspects of life, not just work, according to @autism_sketches.

Sexuality (Gate 59) and **emotional intimacy** (Gate 6) may also change in higher frequency humans, since the purely physical side of sex or mating becomes less important to them. These two gates form the **Channel of Connecting/Mating**, which links the life force energy from the sacral chakra (labeled as "2" below) to the emotional solar plexus chakra (3A, below).

When a person with Gate 59 meets someone with Gate 6, there is an instant connection and magnetism between them, because this channel connects them. We may have one or both gates in our energetic blueprint or none at all, which gives rise to some variations in how we may relate to others (see "Spiritual Guide To Our Relationships").

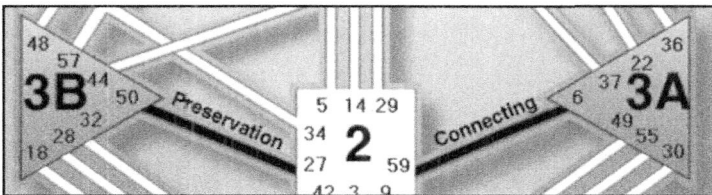

Gate 59 (sacral chakra) provides sexual energy to bond with a mate using different strategies (e.g. pursuer/pursued, bold/shy, promiscuous/not, friend/not, seducer/not, soul mate/aloof). At the shadow level, it is expressed as dishonesty or distrust of others. At a higher level, it is seen as intimacy. At the highest level, it is transparency or being open and honest with self and others.

Gate 6 (solar plexus chakra) is about resolving conflicts or meeting people halfway, which leads to diplomacy and peace. Its lower expression is seen as a fear of intimacy or feeling like a victim of strong passionate emotions that can impact others with friction or peacemaking.

Autistics have a spectrum of sexual expression. They may be *asexual* (with low/no interest in sex), *aromantic* (with low/no attraction toward any gender), *demisexual* (with attraction only via an emotional bond) or *greysexual* (with attraction and desire sometimes, but not usually) or express variations of LBGTQ1A+. Their "love language" includes sharing information about a special interest, being alone together or engaging in parallel playtime or offering support through gestures of friendship, according to @autism_sketches.

Their **emotional life** may also be changed by their **emotional solar plexus (3A) chakra**. For example, they may have *alexithymia* or difficulty identifying some emotions (e.g. fear, anger, jealousy), or describing, expressing or communicating feelings, or differentiating between bodily sensations and emotions. They may identify certain emotions (e.g. joy), but not others (e.g. fear, anger). Their emotions may be active in the body, but they cannot feel or perceive them properly.

This is probably due to their half-human/half-hybrid energetic blueprint that may give them a diluted experience of the emotional range that humans normally experience on this planet. Earth is called the "planet of emotion." This is where souls can experience a wider emotional range (i.e. the highest highs and the lowest lows) than anywhere else in the universe. That makes human lifetimes more challenging, but it also makes us evolve faster (Chapter 1).

When autistics encounter intense emotions, a confrontation or fight/flight situation, they may have a smile or uncontrollable *nervous laughter*, which is a defense mechanism and a sign of distress or panic. They are trying to protect themselves from feeling overwhelm with anxiety. This may become an automatic go-to response in anxiety-inducing circumstances. On the other hand, a *passive face* for autistics can mean internal happiness and excitement. That's why they are often misjudged as being cold, unfeeling or lacking in compassion (see @autism_sketches).

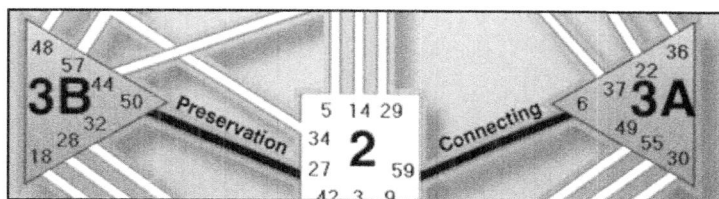

The **fear patterns in the splenic (3B) chakra** are common in both neurotypical and autistic people. They include the fear of inadequacy (Gate 48 Talent/Wisdom), fear of the future (Gate 57 Instinct/Intuition), fear of the past (Gate 44 Alertness/Patterns), fear of responsibility (Gate 50 Values/Stability), fear of failure (Gate 32 Continuity/Endurance), fear of death (Gate 28 Risk Taker/ Game Player) and fear of judgment (Gate 18 Correction/ Perfection).

All of us can relate to these fears, which need not paralyze us. They are usually transient (as a built-in survival mechanism to a threat, e.g. dark alley, bear) and can be overcome by trusting your intuition, listening to your body and taking care of yourself with rest or re-centering.

These are just some of the challenges that autistic people can experience in their five chakra system. Generally, their upper chakras tend to be overexpressed (overactive), while the lower chakras may be underexpressed. They are trying to bridge the physical "3D" world with their innate "5D" world, which is challenging, but not a "developmental disorder" as such.

Most of us have seven major chakras in our bodies, so we experience life in a very different way (Chapter 2). At some point in the future, all humans will evolve to have composite chakras like autistics — maybe not in this lifetime, but in a future lifetime, when we come in as higher frequency humans, who won't have to bridge 3D and 5D the way autistics do right now. Why? Because the Earth environment and humanity as a whole will be higher frequency as well.

Number of souls: In some cases of autism, the number of souls in the person's body may vary. Usually, we have one soul per body, but sometimes two souls want to come into the same body to experience things together. One of them is the primary soul ("driver") and the other soul is supposed to be a passive observer that sometimes becomes a disturbing "backseat driver" (see Chapter 11).

Timing of condition: There are versions of autism that can be seen right at birth and other versions that manifest some time after birth. The baby could be born perfectly normal, but the special energy system is present and will manifest later in childhood, just as planned by the soul. All is choice from the soul's perspective.

Chemical imbalance: In a few cases of autism, a cocktail of chemicals found in polluted air, food, water or ground (e.g. pesticides, herbicides, etc.) or vaccines may affect the child. The chemicals change the way the DNA and RNA work with the energetic templates that create the child's body. From the energetic perspective, the human form is still developing up to the seventh year of life. Any chemicals that are introduced into it during this period will affect the way the child's energy system works and how the gross physical form interacts with it.

The result may be that the *child's frequency is lifted higher*, which changes their behavior. The *soul* in the child's body might actually want to have that higher frequency experience, but the parents might not like it, so they may blame the vaccines or other reasons for the condition.

Who are some famous people with ASD? There are many famous people on the spectrum, such as Michelangelo, Newton, Einstein, Mozart and other historical figures. In our lifetime, many musicians, actors, comedians, writers, athletes, scientists, and business leaders have been diagnosed as having ASD. Certain characters depicted in movies (e.g. *Rainman, The Social Network, Mozart and the Whale*, etc.) and TV shows (e.g. *The Good Doctor, Parenthood, The Office,* etc.) are also helping to educate the public about this condition.

One such role model is Greta Thunberg, who is an autism activist, since she has Aspergers, OCD and selective mutism. She is showing us that you don't need to be a grown up or an adult to be knowledgeable and authoritative beyond her years. She is a climate and environmental activist — an **eco-warrior** with Gate 38 (The Fighter/ Fighting for What is Right), who provokes us through Gate 39 (Provocateur/Re-Calibration) to create some tension in a polite, composed, persistent and dedicated way, so that we change the way we operate on this planet — how we treat the planet and all the living entities on it (below).

"Fighting for climate justice is also fighting for democracy. Our civilization will be increasingly threatened as the planet destabilises, putting everything at risk including democracy. This is a major threat. Democracy is everything. We can't save the living planet without it."
— Greta Thunberg

She is one of the twelve "White Children," who will incarnate at an ascended master level to help us elevate the overall frequencies of humanity over the next 50-70+ years (see "Spiritual Guide To Our Awakening"). She is here to be of service to all of us. Thank you for being here!

Why are Awe-tistics here? They are here to **teach us a new way of being human**. They are here to push our buttons and to take us away from our cheating, competing and warring ways. They are also teaching us about self-love, because we find it easier to give love to children than to ourselves. They are totally innocent, trusting and truthful. They have no agenda except to teach us to accept others as they are and to give them unconditional love.

They are serving us in many ways besides bringing higher frequencies to our Earth plane. They come in with a completely innocent level of understanding of how to be here. They speak the truth — they don't know how to lie. They don't know how to connive, contrive or coerce, because they are totally and utterly above and beyond all of that stuff, according to Needler.

They have difficulty in working in this environment, where everybody has their own agenda to compete and achieve more things. That's why they may struggle to work here, but people who are more awake and aware will naturally communicate with them on other channels (Chapter 3).

When we become more connected, we will operate in a more communal sense as well. We can experience this, when we meditate together, where our combined energies are amplified exponentially based on the number of people participating in the group. Eventually, that will be our natural condition, rather than having to dip into it like we do now, according to Needler.

What's the point? I hope you have a new understanding of autism spectrum disorder, which is an umbrella term for many different conditions that can arise in many ways to fulfill the chosen life plans of various souls. Remember that children are BIG, brave co-creator souls in little bodies. It's a different way to incarnate here, not a "developmental disorder" as such.

Some people are alarmed that ASD is becoming more common without realizing that these "awe-tistic" children are coming in with a higher operating system to teach us a new way of being. They are serving us, just like the other spiritually advanced children (e.g. indigo, crystal, rainbow children and their hybrid combinations, and the White children) that are incarnating in greater numbers than ever before (see "Spiritual Guide To Our Awakening"). That's the plan.

The goal is to raise our frequency, to adjust our vibration to match theirs, not to try to make them into mini-me's of us, as Nora Herold noted. All of us are seeking the same energy in life, which is to be loved, accepted and cared for, to be seen, heard and understood, to be appreciated, safe and supported. That's what we all need to be and do for each another.

"When I was younger I was looking for this magic meaning of life. It's very simple now. Making the lives of others better, doing something of lasting value. That's the meaning of life, it's that simple." – Temple Grandin

CHAPTER 11

WHAT IS THE ENERGETIC BASIS OF BIPOLARISM?

Earth is called the "planet of emotion" for a reason. This is where souls can experience the widest range of emotions — the highest highs and the lowest lows — than anywhere else in the universe. That makes our lifetimes more challenging, but it also makes our souls evolve faster.

Why? Because we have so many different states of "beingness" to play with — not just black and white but all the shades of gray in between. We come here to learn about these states first-hand, sometimes through conditions like Bipolar disorder ("bipolarism").

What is the conventional view? Bipolar disorder (or manic-depressive illness) is a *mood disorder* that causes unusual shifts in mood, energy, activity levels, and the ability to carry out day-to-day tasks. Bipolar disorder affects males and females equally.

The onset of symptoms is between 15 and 30 years old (average 25 years). It is a lifelong illness that requires treatment. The cause is unknown, although genetics, stressful life events, brain structure and other factors are thought to contribute to its presentation.

People with bipolar have high and low moods, known as mania and depression, which differ from the typical ups and downs that most people experience. The spectrum of symptoms may be classified as **Bipolar I** (with mania and major depression), **Bipolar II** (with hypomania and major depression) or **Cyclothymia** (with hypomania and minor depression, below).

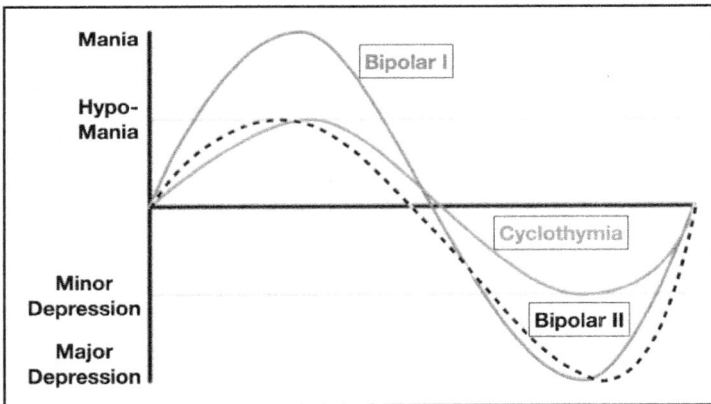

The mood states can also be described by three components: *Activity, Cognition and Emotion*, or the ACE model (see Malhi et al.) as an alternative to standard classification of Bipolar disorder. These components can be *coupled* together, which gives more consistent cycles, because the ACE components are in sync with each other and moving up or down together.

The components can also be *uncoupled* from each other, which can lead to various mixed states (image analogy, below). The severity and duration of symptoms may vary within each of the ACE components, which add their own highs and lows to the overall condition.

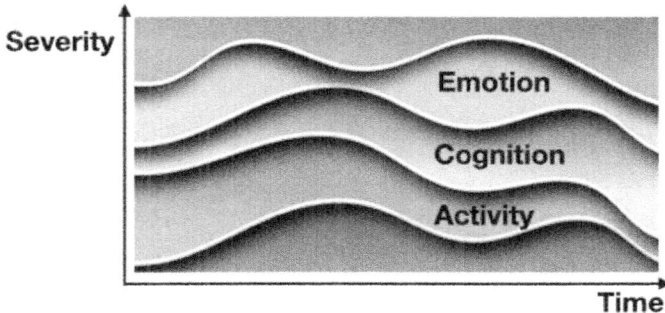

For example, **Activity** at the lower end may include increased or decreased weight, appetite, sleep, fatigue or loss of energy shifting to risk taking behavior, increased energy and activity, decreased need for sleep and increased goal-directed activity at the higher end.

Cognition at the lower end may be seen as psychomotor agitation, decreased ability to think or concentrate, indecisiveness to suicidal plans, thoughts or attempts (lowest point) shifting to agitation, pressured speech, distractibility, inflated self-esteem or grandiosity at the higher end.

Emotions at the lower end may range from feelings of guilt and worthlessness to depressed or irritable moods shifting to expansive moods and racing thoughts at the higher end.

Bipolar symptoms can result in damaged relationships, poor job or school performance, and even suicide. It's a lifelong illness that requires treatment. If left untreated, the symptoms usually get worse. Bipolar disorder can be treated and managed with medications, psychotherapy, self-management strategies. There are additional sources of help and guidance online (e.g. Instagram @this.is.bipolar and @realitybipolardisorder) with coping strategies, support and more.

Note that some people have also had success using the ketogenic diet (see Carrie Brown: Putting bipolar 2 disorder into remission, YouTubeVideo: DietDoctor(dot)com).

What is the energetic basis of bipolarism? The energetic view of this condition is a bit different. It is based on the *soul's perspective,* which can be perceived by energy healers, like Guy Needler ("Psycho-Spiritual Healing"). They have come to realize that our mental disorders are greatly misunderstood, because they have a hidden soul-based component that is often not recognized by doctors, therapists or the individuals themselves. This is new information to us.

In Bipolar disorder — there are two souls in the same body at the same time. The soul and body always work together — think of the *soul* as the driver and the *body* as the car that the soul drives around for a while. In bipolarism, we have two souls driving the same car (image analogy, below).

How can two souls be in the same body? This phenomenon has been going on for thousands of years on Earth and elsewhere. There is an agreement between two or more souls, who want to work together in a particular lifetime. It's just another way to incarnate here, but each case is a unique situation made of different souls that come from different Higher Selves (Chapter 1).

There are lots of people, who have more than one soul in their body. According to Needler, about **54% of the population have two souls in their body**, but the vast majority (90%) of them don't know it. They are not consciously aware of it. There are more souls that want to incarnate than human bodies available for them to use. That's why some souls agree to share the human experience for a while. Many souls wanted to come here at this time in our evolution, when we are awakening as a species (see "Spiritual Guide To Our Awakening"). It's a BIG shift.

From the soul's perspective, it doesn't matter if you are **born** into a body or walk into it later on — that's what we call a "**walk-in**." Most people associate a walk-in with a *soul transfer* or a swap of one soul that leaves for another soul that comes into the same body to continue that life. That is different from **bipolarism** where we have *two or more souls* occupying the same body.

Which soul is in charge? Usually, it is based on the *soul agreement* — it is not unplanned or random. One of the souls is the primary soul, the "driver" that animates the body by integrating with the Tan tien area in the abdomen (see Chapter 2). The secondary soul is usually a passive observer or backseat passenger, who sometimes becomes a disruptive "backseat driver."

Both souls exist within the *same energy set* and experience the same interactions that the physical body is having. But the secondary soul isn't able to affect the body or its environment, because it's not integrated at the Tan tien. Usually, that's the difference between the two souls.

When does it happen? A walk-in can happen *at any time* from before birth to just before death. It depends on what kind of agreement they made before incarnation, when the entry point(s) become available to move in, and which type of walk-in condition is being used.

They can time it, so that one or both souls come in at birth (below). Some souls only want to be here for a short while and go through the gestation or childhood period. Other souls prefer to skip the childhood phase (e.g. being in diapers, learning to walk, talk, etc.) and walk-in to an adult body to be on the planet at a certain point in history.

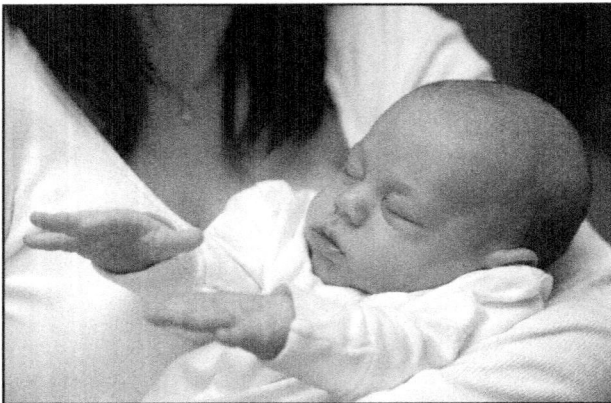

What other factors affect bipolarism? Every case is different, because of various factors affecting the souls, including their soul age, frequency level, sentience level, and role played.

For example, there are five different *soul ages* that differ in their orientation and focus, positive and negative aspects, cultural settings, etc. (see "Spiritual Guide To Our Awakening"). You can have a walk-in of a "young soul" with less experience or an "older soul" with more skills and overall experience that can be shared within the body (below).

| Young soul | Older souls |

They can come in as *standard frequency* human souls or as *higher frequency* souls (indigo, rainbow, crystal and their hybrids) or a mix of both. They can also come in as "backfill people," whose *lower* sentient level (80%) is between that of humans (100%) and animals (50%). Some of our political leaders (e.g. US, UK) are backfill people with two or more backfill souls in them. We may notice some changes in these leaders, when they are giving a speech, acting erratically or making poor decisions (see "Spiritual Guide To Our Awakening").

The souls can take turns being the designated *driver* (active) or the *passenger* (passive). Sometimes they stick to the original agreement made prior to incarnating. Sometimes the passive soul thinks they can do a better job than the active soul, which can lead to arguments and power struggles over command and control of the body (below). Who gets to drive the car!?

The souls can be *temporary* and stay for two minutes, two hours, two years or two decades or they can be *permanent* and stay for the rest of the lifespan of the human vehicle. All is choice.

What are the signs of a walk-in? There are several signs that may be sudden or gradual that may indicate a walk-in event. If a person has a profound *personality change* that keeps changing regularly or has recognizable *mood swings* on a regular basis for any period of time, then it is suggestive of a "**walk-in**" condition where a different personality is taking control of the body.

Here is a brief summary of the types of walk-ins possible in bipolarism:

Planned walk-in by two souls that have agreed to do a one-on-one soul exchange during an incarnation. They will continuously swap in and out of the body to experience the same lifetime as two different souls. The body is controlled by only *one soul at a time*, but the same two souls keep cycling in and out of it. The psychological effects may include loss or shift in memories, loss of time, dissociative states or disorientation and changes in personality, traits and/or habits.

Sequential walk-ins by many souls. The same body can be used by multiple souls that take turns or rotate to *go in and out* of the same body, which is occupied by only *one soul at a time*. Each soul may stay for just a few hours, days or weeks and then swap out with another soul. The psychological effects include some disorientation and changes in personality, traits and/or habits that are usually noticed by others, not by the person who is immersed in their incarnation.

Simultaneous walk-ins by many souls. One body is shared by multiple souls that want to work together. They may come in *one-by-one* at planned intervals or *all at once* to work as an integrated unit. Sometimes this shuffling can affect the life plan. Why? Because multiple souls can play *active* (animating) or *passive* (non-animate) roles on a *permanent* or *temporary* basis.

The number of souls participating in this scenario may be indeterminate, which leads to many variations. Whenever one soul decides it has done enough and leaves, another soul may come in to take its place. The psychological effects depend on how many souls play the *active* role to animate the body and change the personality, traits and/or skills in a noticeable way.

By the way, this condition is often seen in people with a worldwide mission (e.g. presidents, spiritual leaders). Each soul contributes its special skills and talents (e.g. leadership, charisma, diplomacy, communication, etc.) that help the leader in that lifetime.

For instance, Abraham Lincoln (below) had a *temporary walk-in,* where his primary soul was still there, but a secondary soul came to work in tandem with it to give him some extra skill sets, charisma and leadership qualities to help him. The secondary soul was hidden to those who interacted with him. This is not uncommon with our leaders, according to Guy Needler.

Temporary walk-ins can create many variations. In some cases, the temporary soul plays an *active* (animating) role, which means they have the ability to control the body either in isolation or in parallel or in tandem with the primary soul — all these situations create different variations. As a result, there may be notable changes in personality, decision making, specialties or skill sets, particularly if there is a "power struggle" among the souls trying to animate the body.

If the primary soul maintains control of the body and the temporary soul plays a passive (non-animating) role, then no psychological changes will be noted and no treatment is needed. That's how most people with two souls in them operate. It's not noticeable at all.

Stolen vehicle walk-in is a transient condition that can happen when a person gets drunk or takes drugs that make the physical body intolerable to the soul because of the low frequencies. The soul ejects out of the intoxicated body, while the drugs are still in the system. The soul may have a "good trip" or a "bad trip" (see Chapter 15).

That "trip" leaves the body open to attachment by an "Earth bound" soul (who refuses to leave after death and stays in the lower astral level) or an opportunistic energetic astral entity (that is not sentient like a soul). They "steal" the body by briefly latching onto it. The walk-in soul tries to "live" in it (often seen as angry or violent behavior). The astral entity tries to get energy from it until the original soul comes back to the detoxed body once the drugs wear off.

To sum up, a person could be diagnosed as **bipolar**, if they have two souls continuously swapping places, or multiple souls rotating in/out of the body occupied by one soul at a time, or multiple souls in the same body at the same time. All these conditions may result in notable personality changes or mood swings on a regular basis (e.g. once a day/once a week/once a month/once every six months, etc.). It can be subtle or very obvious. Each case is different.

Note that some people diagnosed as "bipolar 2" have only *one soul* in the body. The person may be spiritually awake and highly expansive, but is experiencing uncontrolled movement through the frequencies that creates a sort of "*functional bipolarism*" with euphoria at the higher end and deep depression at the lower end. They may have fear and anxiety when feeling the higher frequencies, because they anticipate the drop and the subsequent depression.

The higher up they go, the lower they potentially drop, if they don't know how to hold their frequency steady at a tolerable or good average range. The goal is to be aware of the embodied experience in the human form, while not losing touch with the soul's energetic side of life. One way to cope with this situation is to practice daily "**Chakra Opening Exercises**" or the moment the person feels they are about to drop down the frequencies (see Appendix).

What do prescription drugs do? There are many types of drugs that are used to control the symptoms of bipolar disorder. Every person has their own unique response and tolerance of these medications. Generally, the drugs create an "energetic disharmony" in the body, which the souls cannot tolerate, according to Guy Needler ("Psycho-Spiritual Healing").

It is like drugging the body to the point, where it is constantly intoxicated and abhorrent to the souls in the body. The drugs reduce the souls' interaction with the body, but they are not driven totally out of it. They eject themselves to sit in the energetic plane or the energies above the head at frequency levels 8, 9 and 10 (image analogy, below).

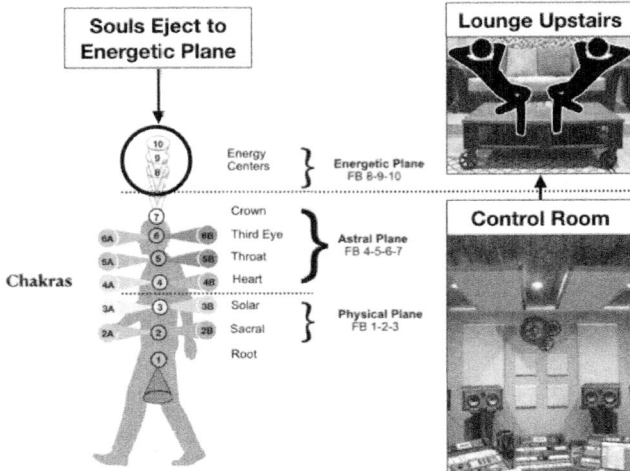

They are still within the sphere of energy that creates the human vehicle, but levels 8-9-10 don't have any chakras or auric layers associated with them, so they don't have the same level of control or connectivity with the body as in the physical level (FB 1-3) or astral levels (FB 4-7).

It's like driving the two souls out of the control room to sit in a lounge upstairs, where they are not able to control the seven chakras or energy centers of the body at FB 1-7 (above).

Note: This doesn't mean you should stop taking your medications that control your bipolar symptoms. This information is meant to help you understand the nature of the condition, and is not to be used or relied upon for any diagnostic or treatment purposes. Please consult your own healthcare provider for all decisions about your case, which is different from everybody else.

What is the energy healing approach? Guy Needler ("Psycho-Spiritual Healing") is a highly experienced healer, who explained why energy healing may be beneficial.

First, the psycho-spiritual healer or therapist (e.g. Quantum Healing Hypnosis Technique or QHHT created by Dolores Cannon) can *communicate with all the souls* at the same time to **get an agreement** among them. The primary soul is allowed to be the only "driver" to animate the vehicle, while the passive souls will go back to being passive observers ("passengers"). The goal is to avoid arguments and power struggles, so that the incarnation will be successful.

Secondly, a very good healer can also *interact with the body energetically* from a higher level. They can reassign the souls by **compartmentalizing** them, as described by Needler in "Psycho-Spiritual Healing." He puts the primary soul into the control room and "herds" the other souls one by one into separate rooms, where they have a clear view the control room, but cannot affect its functions. The *primary soul* is a golden orb, which is more integrated with the human vehicle, whereas the other souls are darker, less integrated and easy to identify. The primary soul cannot see the other souls in the adjacent rooms, so they cannot influence it in any way. This is how the proper roles are re-established among the compartmentalized souls.

Thirdly, sometimes the healer needs to **remove a walk-in soul** from the body, if it was not planned or if it is no longer required by the primary soul. He said the primary and walk-in souls may appear as human forms or as energetic "orbs" in the control room. He herds the unwanted walk-in to a small temporary room, which he uses to transport the walk-in soul back to its own Higher Self, which reabsorbs it into its sentient mass. The patient's normal personality will return, because its soul is no longer distracted by the unwanted walk-in soul. Good riddance!

Note: If you are interested in getting a Healing by Guy Needler, here is a link to his website: BeyondtheSource.org (see Healing tab).

What's the point? I hope this information gives you a newer understanding of bipolar disorder from the perspective that two or more souls may be associated with the same physical body. It is clear that every case of bipolarism is different from others for many reasons.

That may explain the variation in the onset, severity and type of symptoms, which may be related to the number of souls involved, their evolutionary level, and the type of walk-in contract they agreed upon before incarnation, and all the other factors described in this chapter.

Interestingly, many famous people from diverse fields (arts, science, politics, etc.) have been affected by bipolar disorder. Whether conscious of it or not, it may have brought them some extra skill sets, creative abilities or genius along with the potential challenges associated with having more than one soul occupying the same body (below).

Clearly, we have a lot more to learn about this and many other mental conditions.

"Being a healer is being of service. It is both an honor and a great responsibility." — Guy Needler

CHAPTER 12

WHAT IS THE ENERGETIC BASIS OF SCHIZOPHRENIA?

The death of mathematician John F. Nash and his wife, who were immortalized in the movie *"A Beautiful Mind,"* brings us to take a look at schizophrenia, which is another misunderstood condition, according to Guy Needler ("Psycho-Spiritual Healing").

What is the conventional view of schizophrenia? The word "schizophrenia" literally means a splitting of the mind. It is a chronic, severe, and disabling brain disorder that has affected people throughout history.

It occurs at similar rates in all ethnic groups around the world, and affects men and women equally. About 1% of Americans have schizophrenia. Symptoms usually start between ages 16 and 30, a little earlier in men than in women. It is rarely seen in children or adults over age 45. The cause of schizophrenia is unknown. It is a "brain disease" affected by factors, such as genetics, immune or autoimmune dysfunctions, prenatal exposure to viruses, toxins, malnutrition, or taking mind-altering drugs as a youth before brain development is complete (e.g. hallucinogens, cannabis, cocaine, opioids, alcohol, etc.).

People with the disorder may lose touch with reality and have difficulty understanding what is real and what is not, which is *psychosis*. The symptoms include *hallucinations* (seeing, hearing, tasting or smelling things that others cannot see, hear or sense) and *delusions* (false beliefs of persecution, someone reading their minds, controlling their thoughts or making them do things).

They may sit for hours without moving or talking, and seem perfectly fine until they start talking with disorganized speech, thinking or bizarre behavior. They may become withdrawn, disinterested in daily life, school or work, depressed, addicted to drugs or alcohol, suicidal or terrified and agitated by their uncontrolled thoughts.

No two people are exactly the same on the *schizophrenia spectrum*. They may also have other health issues (e.g. smoking, obesity, type 2 diabetes, etc.). It is a serious disabling mental illness that usually requires lifelong treatment with medications, therapy and other support systems.

John Forbes Nash, Jr. was a schizophrenic whose his life story was told in the movie, *"A Beautiful Mind."* He heard "voices" that he thought were a little different from aliens, more like angels. He said he knew it was really his subconscious talking. He came here to teach us about schizophrenia and to give his unique insights into game theory, chance and decision making inside complex systems, because he faced that in his inner and outer world every day. He was the only person who was awarded the Nobel Prize in Economics and the Able Prize in Mathematics.

"I would not dare to say that there is a direct relation between mathematics and madness, but there is no doubt that great mathematicians suffer from maniacal characteristics, delirium and symptoms of schizophrenia.

Though I had success in my research both when I was mad and when I was not, eventually I felt that my work would be better respected if I thought and acted like a 'normal' person." – John F. Nash, Jr. (1928-2015)

What is the energetic basis of schizophrenia? Guy Needler is the first person to shed light on schizophrenia from the *soul's perspective*. He said the condition we call schizophrenia can result from being very open to having an **increased bandwidth of perception**. This allows the person to pick up all sorts of communications on telepathic levels (image analogy, below).

It's a bit like having virtual reality goggles built-in to the person's head and wearing them all day every day (below). They may be physically present in one reality with some people, but for a period of time their consciousness is split away from their body and focused on another reality.

It would look like the person is out of touch with their current reality. They may appear lifeless, apathetic or silent. But actually they are in the other reality that the people around them cannot perceive or interact with.

The problem is the person doesn't have *conscious control* over the level of connectivity or the reality shifting process, so it appears random to them. It can be confusing, overwhelming and intoxicating at the same time (image analogy, below).

Most of us find it very difficult to operate in this way, because we can only handle *one reality* at a time. Our mind has all kinds of filters and barriers ("programming") to block out these other realities. Why? We came here to be in linearity, so we exist in a **linear reality**.

We see things as a finite *series* of events (like going from dot to dot) rather than a *collective* of events (seeing all dots at once). We think we exist on one "timeline" (or event stream) that goes from start to finish, but we can't remember where it all started and don't know where it will end. There is more than one linear path — there are countless timelines/event streams to choose from, and each gives a slightly different experience (see "Spiritual Guide To Our Multiverse").

Your personal reality is based on where *you* choose to focus your consciousness at any now moment (Chapter 15). We do this individually and collectively. We may experience some things by ourselves in a small individualized reality bubble. We may also experience other things with a small group or a whole collective of people that share a larger reality together at the local, planetary, global or universal levels (image analogy, below).

Event Space Levels

Individual   Local   Global   Universal

We have some collective agreements about the circumstances that create the environment that we experience together. This is how we experience everything — it's just that most of us wear "blinders" that block out all the other realities from our conscious awareness in human form.

What kinds of realities can some people access? There are three different situations to consider in people who have access to one or more alternate realities or event spaces, based on the work of Guy Needler ("Psycho-Spiritual Healing"):

Parallel selves: This refers to somebody who is in connectivity with **parallel selves** of themselves in parallel conditions. Most people don't realize this, but we exist in numerous parallel versions of ourselves, which split off every time we make a decision to go one way or another way in life. If our soul is curious about exploring more than one *"what if scenario"* or possibility, then we will explore them as parallel selves in alternative realities to gain more experience from the same lifetime (image analogy, below). It's more efficient that way.

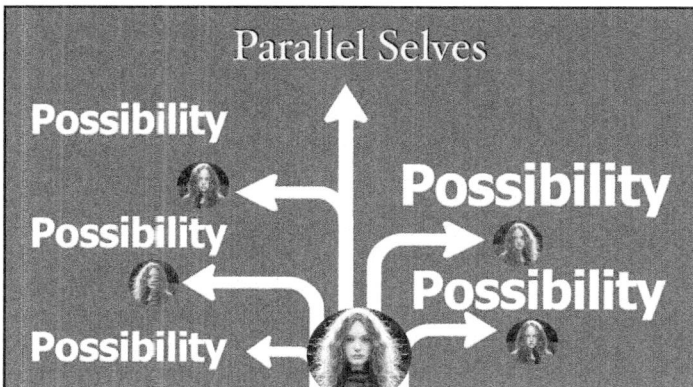
Parallel Selves
Possibility
Possibility
Possibility
Possibility
Possibility
Possibility

Psychics are people who are able to see the "future" or downstream functions of a particular decision. How? They are able to project their consciousness into the other "possibilities" or event spaces where their own parallels are experiencing something, but they also stay *anchored* in their current reality. They can tell others something about that alternative reality, so they seem to have psychic abilities, which is one of the higher intuitive functions (see Chapter 3).

In **schizophrenia**, the person may be able to see, experience or communicate with their own parallel selves in other event spaces or alternative realities, which are as real as the current reality they are in with the people who question their sanity.

The problem is they experience those realities in an *uncontrollable way*, so they have a hard time anchoring themselves to the current reality, where their family, friends, or associates interact with them. They move their consciousness from one reality to another and experience them as if they are just one event space, not many different event spaces with different scenarios playing out. This gives rise to so-called "continuity errors" that create profound *psychological issues*.

Needler said these people have a lot of difficulty in working with their roles and tasks in their current reality, because they will not know what their reality is, how valid it is, and whether their memories are real or fiction. In this case, they run a great risk of being institutionalized (as happened with John Nash often against his will).

Soul Mates: This refers to somebody who is experiencing one or more lives of their soul mates that are projected from the **same Higher Self** as their soul. That's what soul mates are. Some of these soul mates could be human, but living in different parts of the world as younger or older people with a different gender, race, physical characteristics, family, career, etc.

Their lives could also be elsewhere in the universe as any species — including humanoid, alien, or purely energetic forms and at different frequency levels, not just gross physical levels. If they are higher frequency entities, they would appear like "angels" or bright/white beings to us. All these lives are happening simultaneously or in "nowness" (image analogy, below).

In this case, the person moves their consciousness randomly or uncontrollably from one reality to another and experiences them as different scenarios playing out. Some of the alien forms, environments and interactions could be sensed as being frightening or confusing to the person who doesn't understand who these entities are and why it is happening to them.

Most of us are blocked by our mind's "programming" from seeing these soul mates and alternative realities, because they are confusing to humans used to living in a linear reality.

Walk-ins: This refers to somebody who has several souls using the same body, which is the shared vehicle walk-in (Chapter 11). The person may able to see, hear or sense more than one walk-in soul's experiences, which can be confusing and disorienting to them. This is also the basis of *bipolar disorder* with two souls in one body (Chapter 11) and *multiple personality disorder* that can have up to seven souls in one body (image analogy, below).

Two or More Souls

It's no wonder people can get confused by these different realities. Needler has treated people diagnosed as schizophrenics from different parts of the world. He gave two examples of his psycho-spiritual healings, which are customized to the person's specific situation.

Case Study #1: Young male – Parallel selves version

Needler met a disoriented young man, who was quite a powerful individual in his own right. He had the ability to move between three different parallel lives in three different realities. But the young man had no control over that level of connection, so it was both overwhelming and intoxicating to him at the same time. He wanted to be able to control it, but he couldn't. He developed anxiety, worry, depression, lack of confidence and frustration with his family.

To heal him, Needler had to educate the person as to what was happening with these different realities. He had work with all three parallel versions of the man and shut things down in certain ways (e.g. severing the energetic links between the patient and his two parallel selves in other event bubbles), so that the person could anchor himself to one reality. Afterwards the person felt grief, when he lost the connectivity to his parallel selves. He wanted to continue to monitor them, but in a more controlled way, so he's working on developing that ability.

Case Study #2: Young female – Shared vehicle walk-in version

Needler said there are lots of individuals that have more than one soul in their physical form (see Chapter 11). One of them is the primary soul that animates the body, and the other ones are usually passive. He was called to heal a young lady, whose personality changed from one day to the next, because she had three souls in place, all of which played a passive but controlling role in the same human body (shared vehicle).

To heal her, Needler had to communicate with all three souls simultaneously to explain that the body couldn't cope with them rotating through her in that way. He found out that one personality was preferred by the girl's family, so that soul was assigned the primary role and the other two were assigned passive roles, so that the incarnation would be successful.

If you are interested in getting a Healing by Guy Needler, here is a link to his website: BeyondtheSource.org (see Healing tab).

Note: This doesn't mean you should stop taking your medications that control your own symptoms. This information is meant to help you understand the nature of the condition, and is not to be used or relied upon for any diagnostic or treatment purposes. Please consult your own healthcare provider for all decisions about your case, which is different from everybody else.

Who are the schizophrenics among us? There are many famous people from actors to comedians, artists, musicians, athletes and mathematicians, who have been diagnosed with this condition. It may give them something extra for creative activities, like music, new ideas or theories that help all of us evolve.

What's the point? I hope that you have a new appreciation for what we consider to be mental illness, because our current understanding of these conditions is very limited. There is a tendency to overmedicate the patient to mask the symptoms and counter their side effects without a clue about the underlying energetic soul-based condition, which can be affected by various situations that contribute to the schizophrenia spectrum, for instance.

It has been predicted that the biggest problem in this century will not be heart disease or cancer, but mental illness. That's why it's important to be aware that as we ascend to higher frequencies, we will gain more connectivity and functionality (e.g. higher intuitive functions in Chapter 3). That's how our scientists, inventors, musical geniuses and others get their downloads to create something new and different (see "Spiritual Guide To Our Awakening").

But that also means there are potentially more opportunities for some "glitches" to occur in certain people (e.g. children and young people in particular), who are incarnating as higher frequency humans, and who need to be properly diagnosed, educated and healed, not just overmedicated or institutionalized as in the past.

This is where you (as a spiritually aware person) can play an important role in educating and alerting parents, therapists, physicians and healers to a newer understanding of these sorts of conditions, not as a physical "brain disease," but sometimes as a manifestation of accessing higher frequencies and functions that are not yet considered "normal" by our society.

"Perhaps it is good to have a beautiful mind, but an even greater gift is to discover a beautiful heart." — *John F. Nash, Jr.*

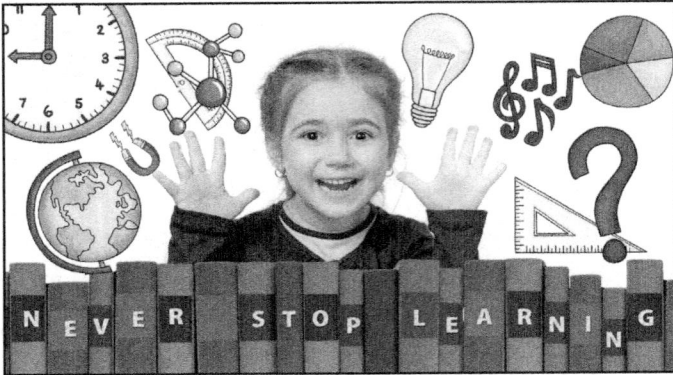

CHAPTER 13

WHAT IS THE ENERGETIC BASIS OF ADD/ADHD?

The terms ADD and ADHD are used interchangeably, although currently it is called Attention Deficit Hyperactivity Disorder. This neurobehavioral condition has been recognized since the late 1700's and affects about 5% of the adult population (over 11 million people) in the U.S.

What is the conventional view of ADHD? The rate of diagnosis of ADHD has increased 5% per year from 2003 to 2011. The cause is unknown, but it tends to run in families. It is about four times more common in boys than in girls. It tends to persist from childhood to adulthood in about half to two-thirds of the individuals.

No two people are exactly the same. Every person has a unique presentation linked to their genetics and brain chemistry, structure, function, metabolism and connectivity with some parts of the brain being overactivated and other parts being underactivated.

There is no cure and most people don't outgrow it. ADHD is recognized as a disability under the Americans with Disabilities Act. Treatment involves a combination of medication to manage brain functions and symptoms and therapy to help with daily coping strategies.

What are the symptoms of ADHD? According to David Rabiner, PhD, the diagnosis of ADHD is based on clinical judgment of a number of neurobehavioral symptoms that must be present for at least 6 months in two or more settings (e.g. home, school, work). He noted that there are many people who believe that ADHD is a medical term inappropriately attached to children who show largely 'typical' behavior (below).

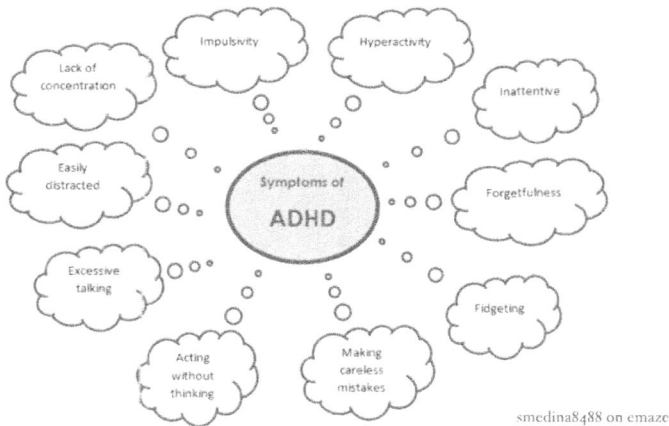

Impulsivity

Hyperactivity

Lack of concentration

Inattentive

Easily distracted

Symptoms of **ADHD**

Forgetfulness

Excessive talking

Fidgeting

Acting without thinking

Making careless mistakes

smedina8488 on emaze

The symptoms may vary depending on the age of the individual (e.g. child, adolescent, adult). There must be clear evidence that they interfere with or reduce the quality of social, academic or occupational functioning. The severity is scored as mild, moderate or severe, but that may change or lessen with age.

There are **three presentations** of ADHD called Predominantly Inattentive, Predominantly Hyperactive-

Impulsive, or Combined — each has its characteristic set of symptoms.

ADHD is often associated with other conditions, such as mood and anxiety disorders. It can also occur with Obesity (Chapter 5), Depression (Chapter 8), Addiction (Chapter 9), Autistic spectrum disorder (Chapter 10), Bipolar disorder (Chapter 11) or Schizophrenia (Chapter 12).

On the other hand, these people can be original and imaginative dreamers, who are creative, observant, inquisitive and inventive as well as resourceful, adaptable, passionate, optimistic, fun and entertaining (below).

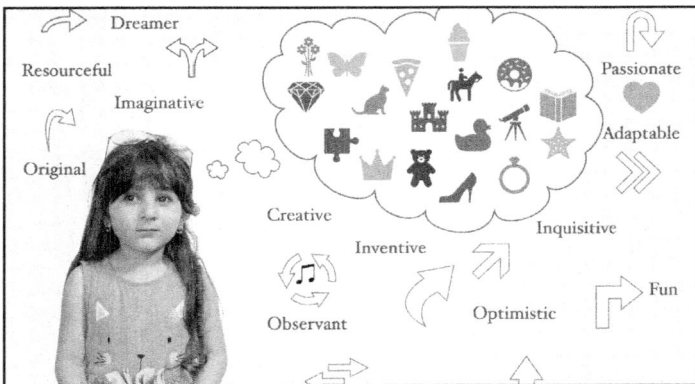

These qualities make them better suited for creative, active or energy work rather than work with deadlines and routines (e.g. office work).

How does the energetic blueprint reflect ADHD? When we look at the energetic blueprint of the body using Human Design (Chapter 3), we can map certain chakras, gates and channels as common elements found in people diagnosed with ADHD.

Our soul chooses which gates to work on at the individual level, but we get exposed to all 64 gates at the collective level, because different people choose different gates to experience, learn and evolve from. They are all around us — unless we're a hermit in a cave or something!?

These gates represent *core human archetypes* or states of **"beingness"** (meaning **thoughts**, **behaviors** and/or **actions**) rather than a state of physicality. Each gate describes a wide spectrum of frequencies from the lowest lows (shadows or victim states) to average levels to the highest highs seen in enlightened beings (e.g. Jesus, Buddha). We use these gates to experience, learn and evolve within the physical universe, where the polar opposites of black and white and all the shades of grey in between are played out in many creative ways (below).

Black   White

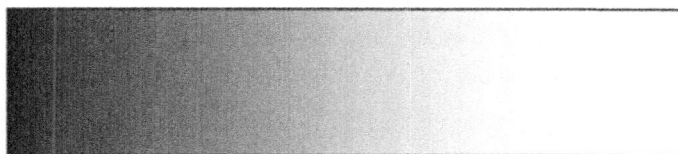

According to Karen Curry ("Understanding Human Design"), there is nothing wrong with the children diagnosed as ADHD. She said some "attention deficit" and "hyperactive" behaviors can be explained by examining the children's energetic blueprints.

For example, many of these **"attention deficit"** children have **"Open Minds"**— meaning Open Head/Seventh and Open Mind/Sixth chakras (with commonly found gates circled in red, below). That means they have an **open and flexible mind**, which makes them clever. They can pick up the thoughts of other people before they even speak. They are great *mind readers.*

Open Head/Mind

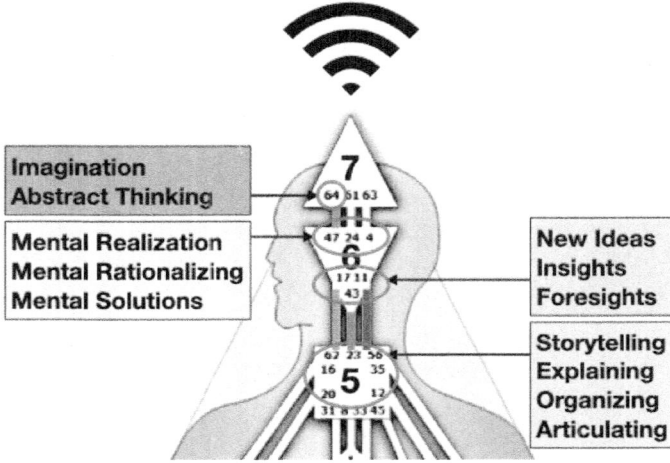

But they can also *amplify* the ideas, thoughts and questions of others, who don't have an Open Head/Mind. That can make them feel scattered, overwhelmed or mentally pressured to answer other people's questions. This is all happening *unconsciously* on the energetic level.

Every gate has a higher and lower expression in its frequency spectrum. For example, many of them have Gate 64 of Imagination/Abstract Thinking that can become confused by all the inputs around their head. It connects with Gate 47 of Realization/Transmutation that can bring "aha moments" about the past or mental anxiety, exhaustion or oppression. Gate 24 of Invention/Rational Thinking can also lead to repeating mind loops/spirals to break the silence in the mind. Gate 4 of Solutions can bring more understanding or a busy mind engaged in endless pursuit of answers for everything (above).

Many also have Gate 11 of Ideas/Concepts, which can be indulged in to escape boredom. It connects with Gate 56 of Stimulation/Storytelling, which can bring curiosity or overstimulation and distraction. Gate 43 of Insights/ Epiphanies can bring deafness (not listening to others) or talking too much (to deafen others), then feeling misunderstood or rejected by them. It connects with Gate 23 of Assimilation/Explanation that can make them blurt out answers or overexplain themselves in complicated ways that make them look like a freak or a genius.

Some have Gate 17 of Foresight/Opinions that connect with Gate 62 of Details/Organization that have the facts to back up their opinions (or not). Gate 12 of Articulation/ Social Caution knows when change is coming, but may speak and act out of turn in their restlessness (above).

Imagine a child with an open mind in a large classroom. All the mental energy projected from the teacher and other students can easily distract them. They can get overstimulated and forget what they are supposed to be focused on. Their challenge is to learn to tell which thoughts and questions come from their own mind vs. somebody else's mind in the room (below). How?

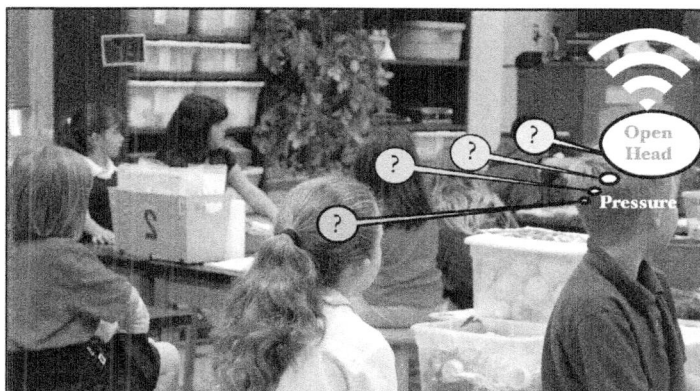

They need to take a break. Things that may help include daily meditation to learn to observe their own thoughts, while being present and calm. Getting their head wet in a shower, pool or body of water also helps to "reset" the circuitry in an overstimulated head (below).

Taking a break from all electronic devices, like TV, video games, tablets, and smartphones will also help, because they entrain us to unnatural frequencies emitted by these devices instead of the natural pulse of the Earth, which is recalibrated by grounding and being outside in nature.

Similarly, their "**hyperactivity**" may relate to an **"Open Root"** center, which is a motor center driven by adrenaline or fight/flight energy (below). In a classroom setting, a child with an open root takes in all the adrenaline energy of the class and *amplifies* it.

They feel a rush of pressure and want to move, sit up, jump or run unexpectedly, because they are driven by an amplified motor and need to release that energy (below).

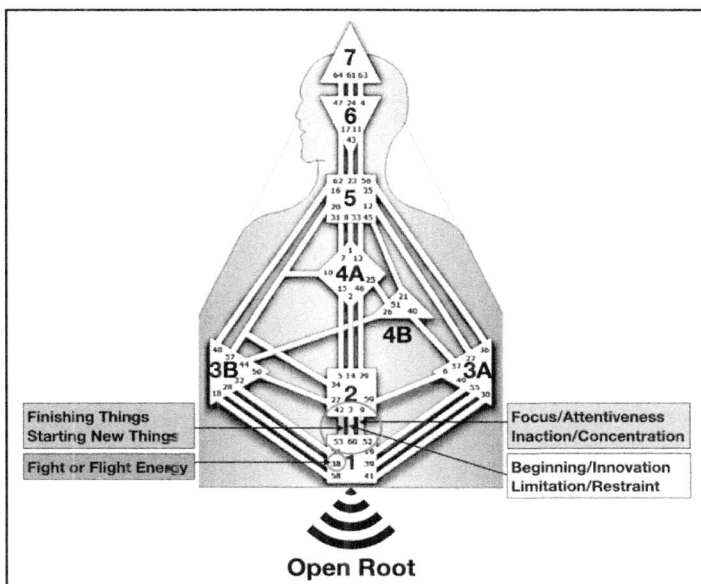

Their challenge is to learn to **ground** themselves. How?

By walking barefoot or lying down on the grass, walking and petting a dog or cat, doing something physical like karate, hopping up and down, going for a hike, and drinking lots of water. All these activities will help move and discharge the energies in the body (below).

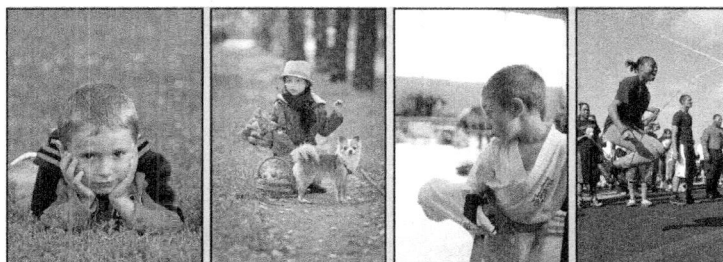

What is the energetic basis of ADHD? Guy Needler ("Psycho-Spiritual Healing") is one of the first people to recognize that conditions like autism, schizophrenia, bipolar disorder and ADHD have an energetic or soul-based component that is not understood by therapists or those affected by the conditions.

He doesn't like to use the terms ADD/ADHD, because it's not really "attention deficit" — it's *hyperattention*, as their attention is on so many different levels.

When he logs into these children, they are one of the newer indigo, crystal, rainbow or hybrid children who are advanced higher frequency beings (see Chapter 10). They are here to increase the collective frequencies of humanity that dropped after the World Wars. These people are born with a spiritually advanced "energy set" — it is how their soul has chosen to incarnate in order to have a different life experience on Earth.

What does that mean? Here is a simple analogy. Most people operate with a standard radio that can tune into three stations (with a slow dial up connection, below, left). We have all kinds of barriers and filter that limit us in this reality.

But those with ADHD have a "supernormal radio" that is always attuned to ten or more stations (with a very high-speed fiberoptic connection). They are open to ultra-high and mega-high frequencies. That makes them operate in a different way.

They have more connectivity than most people (below, right). They can communicate with each other on many energetic levels using emotional, telepathic and other higher functions (Chapter 3).

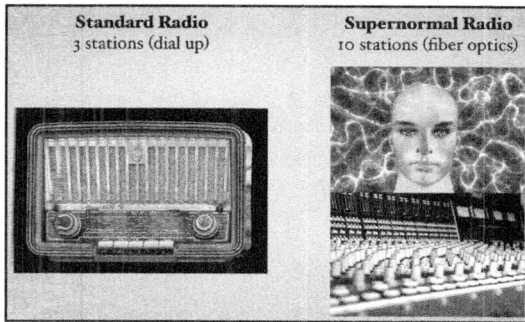

Standard Radio	Supernormal Radio
3 stations (dial up)	10 stations (fiber optics)

But they struggle to communicate with those who don't share their abilities (below). They broadcast information to those around them, but what we give back isn't what they expect, so it can be very frustrating to them. They can't see the point in communicating with us or doing something, when we're not listening to them.

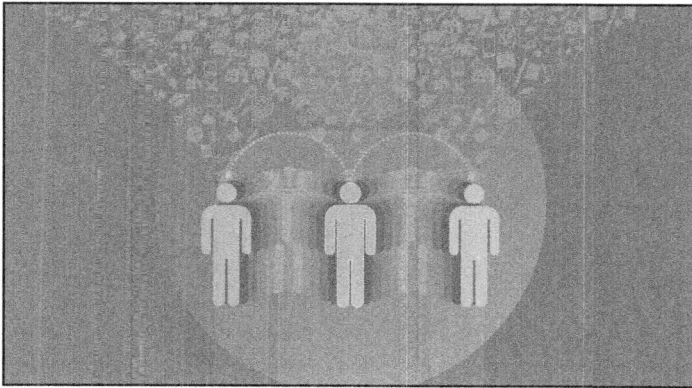

Some try to dumb down their extra sensory perception, so they can operate at our level, or turn off some of their higher functions. Some try to numb themselves with alcohol and drugs to get out of the body (Chapter 9). That makes them ungrounded and not present. They may have a sense of being overwhelmed, having no filters, or always being on edge, because their senses are all open, so they pick up lots of other bits and pieces of information that the rest of us don't.

Most adults with ADHD don't just have ADHD. About 75% to 80% also have disorders, such as major depression, bipolar disorder, anxiety and substance abuse (see KM Antshel et al.).

ADHD tends to run in families and continues into adulthood in half the cases. It may run in families, because those souls wish to incarnate around others with ADHD, who may have learned to manage or cope with their condition in various ways. They are better able to communicate with each other on many levels.

What is the best approach to coping with life? Many with ADHD are given medications, which suppress their natural higher frequency condition, so that they can better integrate with others. But Needler said the best approach is to allow them to be and work with others like them, because they will be able to communicate with each other.

A person speaking or communicating on twelve different frequency levels will be able to communicate with somebody like them on twelve different frequency levels. They will realize that they are not alone and they will start to operate properly. It is also important to educate the patient, their parents and teachers about the energetic basis of this condition to allow a better understanding of it with self-acceptance.

Note: This doesn't mean you should stop taking your medications that control your own symptoms. This information is meant to help you understand the nature of the condition, and is not to be used or relied upon for any diagnostic or treatment purposes. Please consult your own healthcare provider for all decisions about your case, which is different from everybody else.

Who are the hyperattentives among us? There are many famous people from presidents to CEOs, artists, scientists and inventors, who have been diagnosed as having this condition.

They include Abraham Lincoln, Agatha Christie, Albert Einstein, Isaac Newton, Frank Lloyd Wright, Mark Twain, Michael Jordan, Richard Branson, Bill Gates, Henry Ford, Thomas Edison, Vincent van Gogh, Virginia Woolf, John Lennon and others (below).

Whether conscious of it or not, their ability to access higher frequencies means they could channel and download things like music, new ideas or inventions that help us all evolve.

What's the point? I hope this gives you a new perspective on ADHD, which is another poorly understood but increasingly common condition like autism (Chapter

10). It's not a deficit or a "disability," but a different energetic blueprint to take in, process and handle energy and information on our world with more access to higher functions.

Their soul chose to incarnate with this special energy set. It is not caused by too much sugar, video games, bad parenting, etc. It may run in families, because those souls wish to incarnate around others with ADHD, who may have learned to manage or cope with their condition in various ways. They are better able to communicate with each other on many levels.

Clearly, we need to change the way we assess and educate these newer, higher frequency children (labeled as ADHD, autistic, indigo, crystal, rainbow, hybrids, etc.), whose needs among other things may include individualized instruction, smaller classrooms with like students, ways to discharge the amplified energy from their system, and ways to cope with their "openness" to the world around them.

They are here to help the rest of us evolve to higher frequencies. Their numbers will continue to increase over time. The sooner we increase our own frequencies, the easier their life will be. They are here to teach us a new way of being human — a higher frequency human with more connectivity with the greater reality (see "Spiritual Guide To Our Awakening").

"Who you are is an individuation of Divinity. Why are you are here is to demonstrate that." — Neale Donald Walsch

CHAPTER 14

WHAT IS THE ENERGETIC BASIS OF OCD?

Let's take a look at Obsessive Compulsive Disorder (OCD) to compare the conventional vs. energetic perspectives, including some past life patterns that may be influencing this condition.

What is the conventional view of OCD? A condition resembling OCD has been recognized for more than 300 years, according to Wayne Goodman (PsychCentral.com). OCD affects men, women, and children of all races and backgrounds equally. About 1% of adults and 1 in 200 kids and teens have OCD. The highest levels are found in the 18-29 year old group.

The cause of OCD is not known, but there are many theories that include biologic and genetic factors and learned behaviors, such as rituals or avoiding certain things (e.g. heights, germs). In some children infections, such as strep throat may trigger sudden, immune-mediated OCD out of the blue, so the causes may vary from person to person. About 90% of people with OCD have another condition at some point. The **OCD spectrum** includes anxiety or mood disorders, depression, bipolar, attention deficit, autism, Tourette's or other things like hoarding, hair pulling, etc. (below).

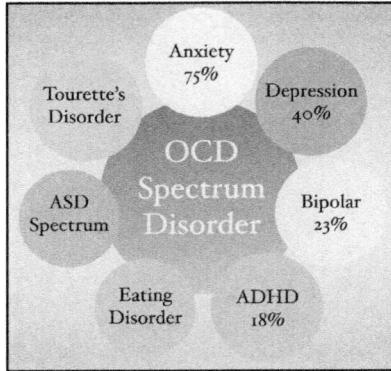

The OCD cycle has four components: intrusive thoughts (obsessions) that lead to anxiety and behaviors (compulsions) that lead to temporary relief from anxiety, then the cycle repeats.

The **obsessions** are unwanted or intrusive *thoughts, mental images* or *urges* that occur over and over again and trigger uncontrollable feelings of anxiety, fear, worry, disgust or doubts.

Some common obsessions are fear of contamination (e.g. germs, bugs, dirt, chemicals), fear of losing control (e.g. harming self/others, violent images, blurting insults, stealing), fear of being harmed (e.g. fire, burglary), perfectionism, getting sick (e.g. cancer), unwanted sexual or violent thoughts (e.g. pedophilia), and religious obsessions ("scrupulosity" about morality, blasphemy, sins, etc.). The obsessions occur over and over again and feel out of control.

The **compulsions** are excessive, repetitive *behaviors* or *mental acts* to try to counteract or make the obsessions go away. Some common compulsions are excess washing and cleaning (e.g. hands, grooming, arranging things), checking (e.g. door locked, oven/appliances turned off), repeating activities (e.g. rewriting, tapping, going in/out doors) or mental compulsions (e.g. thought suppression, reviewing, counting, praying, rituals, etc.). But the relief is temporary.

These obsessions and compulsions take lot of time (>1 hr+/day) and get in the way of daily activities, such as going to school or work, socializing, and spending time with the family. The severity of OCD may range from mild (15%) to moderate (35%) to severe (50% of cases).

From the time OCD first appears, it takes about 14–17 years for people to receive appropriate treatment. The most effective treatments are cognitive behavior therapy (e.g. ERP or exposure to fears and compulsive response prevention with various exercises) and/or various medications (e.g. antidepressants). Some cases may respond to a single dose or microdosing of a medication under supervision (e.g. ayahuasca, psilocybin, ketamine).

Family education and support is important. About 70% of people with OCD will benefit from therapy, medicine or both and helpful support groups (see @ocdawareness and @ocddoodles).

What is the energetic basis of OCD? When we look at the energetic blueprint of the body using Human Design (Chapter 3), it shows us how the life force energy runs throughout the body. We can map certain chakras with certain gates as common elements found in some people with OCD, based on their various symptoms (below).

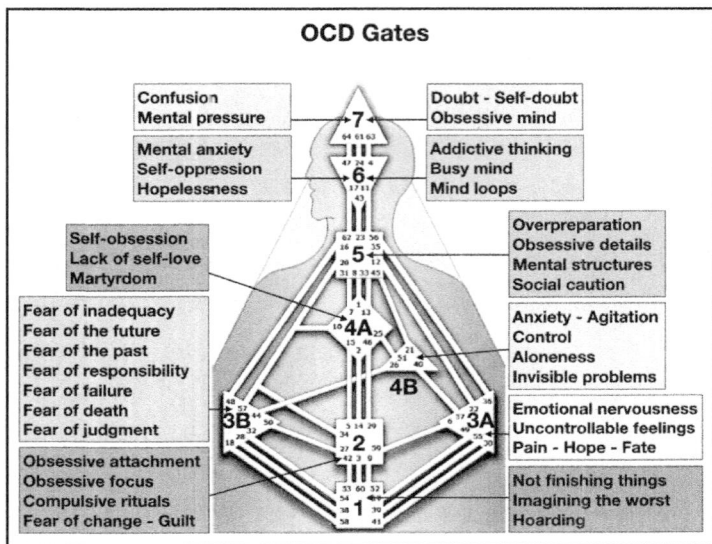

There are 64 gates in total. Our soul chooses which gates to work on at the individual level, but we get exposed to all 64 gates at the collective level, because different people will choose different gates to experience, learn and evolve from in every lifetime.

We work on 26 of them as our soul self and human personality. Each gate represents a totally different state of being that we express as different thoughts, feelings or actions along a **whole spectrum of frequencies** (below).

Our soul wants to experience the whole gradient, not just one point on the spectrum. For example, Gate 50 of Values/Stability may be expressed at the lower end as taking on too much responsibility for the safety and welfare of others, while having intense feelings of guilt at the same time. We may feel overloaded and burned out, while we disregard or become blind to the values that would serve us and others in a more balanced or harmonious way (below).

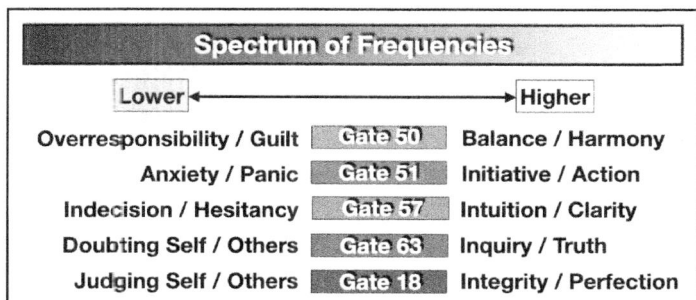

Spectrum of Frequencies		
Lower ◄——————————► Higher		
Overresponsibility / Guilt	Gate 50	Balance / Harmony
Anxiety / Panic	Gate 51	Initiative / Action
Indecision / Hesitancy	Gate 57	Intuition / Clarity
Doubting Self / Others	Gate 63	Inquiry / Truth
Judging Self / Others	Gate 18	Integrity / Perfection

There is nothing wrong with you — it's an experience, but you are not your experience. It's what your *soul* wanted you to experience in human form for a while (not forever).

We are on a hero's journey with some trials and tribulations. The soul evolves from everything we will encounter and attempt to shift, including moving from guilt to balanced responsibility. That's the path of growth and transformation your soul wanted to experience and not be stuck at any point.

Every gate has a specific fear pattern and associated behaviors, which may be found in any person, such as the "fear gates" in the splenic chakra 3B (below).

I CHING GATE Number & Name	FEAR PATTERN	SHADOW	GIFT	SIDDHI
50 Values	Fear of overresponsibility, feeling guilty	Corruption	Equilibrium	Harmony
32 Continuity	Fear of failure, panicking over change	Failure	Preservation	Veneration
26 Integrity	Fear of being deceived, not sharing the truth	Pride	Adaptability	Inner Balance
12 Social Caution	Fear of speaking out, shyness, keeping secrets	Vanity	Discrimination	Purity
45 Rulership	Fear of not being the ruler, not having possessions	Dominance	Synthesis	Communion
16 Skills	Fear of not having enough skills or depth	Indifference	Versatility	Mastery
4 Mental Solutions	Fear of not finding answers or solutions that work	Intolerance	Understanding	Forgiveness
62 Details	Fear of missing details, have obsessive thoughts	Intellect	Precision	Impeccability
18 Correction	Fear of making mistakes, perfectionism	Judgment	Integrity	Perfection
48 Knowledge	Fear of inadequacy, being insignificant	Inadequacy	Resourcefulness	Wisdom

Every person has a *unique blueprint* with a unique combination of gates and channels that may be expressed at various frequency levels ranging from the victim/shadow patterns to gift and siddhi/divine gift levels.

For example, the *fear of making mistakes* or fear of authority or being judged by others leads to perfectionism and self-judgment (Gate 18). The *fear of failure* creates panic and indecision over change (Gate 32) or fear of not meeting your expectations of success, which can keep you stuck in the old mold (Gate 42). The *fear of missing details* can create obsessive focus for details (Gate 9) or checking and rechecking details and being unable to switch off the mind (Gate 62). Similarly, the *fear of ignorance* creates mental anxiety or repetitive thought loops (Gate 24). The *fear of repeating past mistakes* creates hyperalertness to outer patterns and distrust of others (Gate 44), while the *fear of lack/emptiness* may create a hoarder (Gates 39-55, see Chapter 5).

Every gate also has a gift, which is built-in to our blueprint and already within us — we just need to release that gift, which represents the higher expression of the gate.

How? By raising our own *frequency* to meet and embody it (see Appendix, Chakra Opening Exercises).

Think of the **human form** in terms of water that goes from ice to liquid to steam or gas, when we apply heat to it.

The same thing happens with our human form, when we raise our frequency, because it is made of seven energetic templates that create our solid physical form (at frequency bands 1-3), a liquid light body (at FB 4-5) and a gaseous or energetic form (at FB 6-7, below).

Seven Energetic Templates

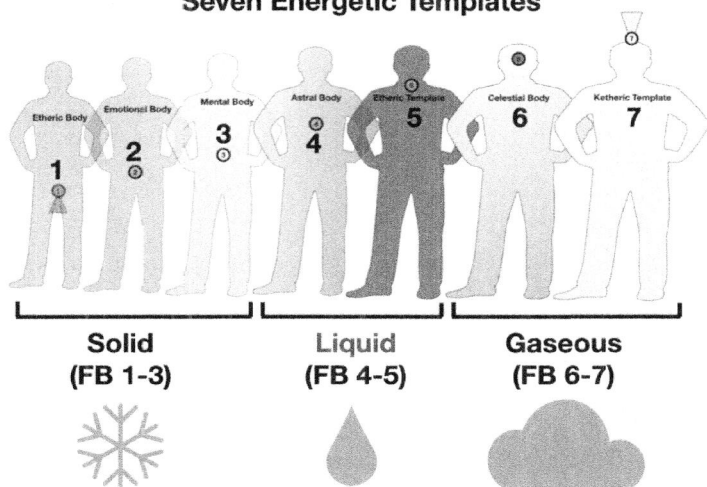

All these templates are already within us — they're part of our exquisitely versatile human form. That's why we know that our soul blueprint doesn't have to doom us. The fear states are at one end of the spectrum and *mastery* is at the other end. We have access to both ends with our *conscious* desire, intention, thought and action (see "Spiritual Guide To Our Universal Laws").

What else may affect the expression of OCD? There are many **past life patterns** that may be carried over to the present life. The circumstances surrounding the fear patterns will vary from person to person, depending on the particulars of their lifetimes (e.g. gender, race, family setting, location, era, circumstances, past lives, future lives, galactic lives, parallel lives, etc.).

Guy Needler ("Psycho-Spiritual Healing") explained more about some features of OCD:

Perfectionism: This is based on the residual memory of the energetic where everything is in perfection. You can create whatever you need instantaneously. It is the desire to make something physical equal that perfection. The problem is the desire for perfection becomes the main link with the energetic, and hence, the focus and subsequent obsession. We try to go back into understanding who and what we are through that obsession, which is perfectionism — whether it is cleaning, looking after the self, self-grooming, trying to find things wrong in documentation, being overly checking and those sorts of things. These things that are obsessional are the link that the soul is trying to maintain with the energetic.

Unwanted sexual thoughts: The sexual side of things isn't anything to do with previous knowledge. It is a function of karma, which is about being addicted to a sensory stimulus or a bliss state associated with the physical level, not because we are missing the energetic bliss state.

Loss of control: This is another memory of being in the energetic, where everything is done instantaneously. There is no reference to anything that can't be done. But losing control is also part of the ego, so it's a mixture of the two — the energetic side and the physical side. When we go into the physical, we lose the ability to be in control of everything that we are, because we have a significantly reduced bandwidth and communicative ability here. That creates the ego, which wants to control things or be in control, so it's a function of being in the physical.

Fear of pandemic: This happens in people, who may have been incarnate during a plague (e.g. bubonic plague, Spanish flu), which wiped out millions of people, because of lack of medical technology or knowledge. This fear also happens in people, who are susceptible to conspiracy theories or reprogramming based on the thoughts of other people. They tend to react badly, because they are not able to control their mortality. It is a karmic effect with the ego.

Fear of death: The fear of death by cancer, fire, water, etc., may also be linked to a past life experience, such as dying in a fire, being burned at the stake, drowning in a sinking boat or in a flood, etc. If you lost all your possessions in a fire or died of starvation, you may hoard food, clothes or even trash, because you want to save things for a rainy day. Things that happened in the past may "bleed through" to create a fear of death in the current life, so you can release it.

People who are always checking things like doors, drawers, locks, etc., may have been guards against enemies or theft who were killed if they didn't do their job properly. Some avoid taking risks in this life, because they had to kill people in a past life. Others may be addicted to extreme sports, gambling, risky things or the adrenaline rush of war or other karmic activities that attach you to the physical plane. All these thoughts and behaviors made sense in a past life, but can become obsessions or compulsions that disempower you in this life.

Religious obsessions: This is using religion as a way of connecting between your Higher Self and Source, as a way home without seeing the potential errors in that level of teaching. There may be a link to previous lives, where they may have been a powerful figure in a religious sect or a controlling body that was based on following a certain way to gain "heaven on earth."

Needler said therapy for OCD is **psycho-spiritual healing** with removal of any past life links and karmic links that attach us to the physical plane. In his experience, taking medication is a short term hit, but not a long term solution for this condition.

Note: This doesn't mean you should stop taking your medications that control your own symptoms. This information is meant to help you understand the nature of the condition, and is not to be used or relied upon for any diagnostic or treatment purposes. Please consult your own healthcare provider for all decisions about your case, which is different from everybody else.

What's the point? I hope this piece helps you see OCD from a different perspective with energetic, past life and egoic influences upon its origin and expression in various forms. Every person is unique and different in terms of their programming, conditioning, soul's goals and evolutionary path. What works for one person may not work for another.

Wendy Kennedy ("The Great Human Potential") said, if you're thinking about the *past*, you will feel shame, guilt or judgment. If you're thinking about the *future*, it's usually about control, trust, security, worry or approval issues. In either case, you're operating from the egoic mind level, not the heart. When you are heart-centered and *present*, you are standing in your full power to make changes in your life (Chapter 15). How?

By *grounding* ourselves into the body and putting ourselves into our *heart center*. The easiest and fastest way to get there is by thinking of something that makes us *smile* (e.g. baby animals, beautiful nature scenes, etc.). We will feel our heart space expanding instantly, but we won't sustain it for long. We'll just need to "reset" ourselves back to the heart throughout the day, because we tend to go back to the mind, which is normal and expected in human form (below).

"In truth, no issue is ever solved at the level of the ego, a.k.a the operating system of the mind. Integration happens from the higher level of consciousness or the operating system of the heart." — Wendy Kennedy

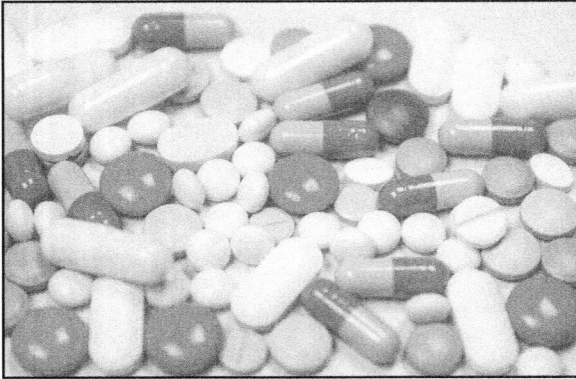

CHAPTER 15

HOW TO BRIDGE SCIENCE AND SPIRITUALITY FOR HEALTH?

"Today's spiritual science is tomorrow's hard science."
— *Guy Needler*

Bridging science and spirituality has been the underlying theme in all of my books. Why? We need to understand how they fit into the Big Picture that integrates both science and spirituality as simply different ways to understand the reality that we and everything around us exists within.

We can use science or *outer technology* to study the bottom 25% of the physical universe or the bottom three frequencies that create our gross physical body. We can't measure the human subtle bodies by scientific means, but we can access them by the *inner technology* within us.

Science helps us make sense of one part of the whole (0.7% of our multiverse) and spirituality helps us understand the rest of the greater reality. We need both perspectives to understand the Big Picture (see "Spiritual Guide To Our Multiverse").

What is meant by outer vs. inner technology? *Science* represents outer technology, because it looks at the outer world in physical or material terms to build new forms, structures, materials, devices and machinery that we use to build physical structures and civilizations. The danger with outer technology is becoming seduced by the abuse or love of power over others.

Science uses the operating system of the *mind* to explain everything. It relies primarily on the left brain that is focused on linear thinking, logical inquiry and experimentation using facts, formulas and patterns to find solutions to problems. This can lead us to a mechanical worldview that excludes anything that cannot be measured or doesn't fit our theories or belief systems.

Spirituality represents our inner technology based on innate energetic processes. It uses the operating system of the *heart* to connect to "superconsciousness" or the Higher Self and Source. This gives us access to higher intuitive and right brain functions with creativity, imagination and a holistic view of life. The danger with inner technology is "spiritual bypassing," where we get cut off from being embodied or being human, which is the whole point of incarnation.

That's why we need both science and spirituality. We are sentient entities having a human experience while evolving through the Material Age, Energy Age, Mental Age and Spiritual Age, the four ages or epochs that create the world cycle that reflects the intellectual and spiritual development of humanity (see "Spiritual Guide To Our Awakening").

What is my story? I call myself a research scientist turned spiritual scientist. Why? I have been curious about science all my life. I wanted to understand living beings by looking within using scientific methods to study the whole animal — its organs, fluids, tissues and cells, how they function, how they develop dysfunctions (e.g. inflammation, infection, cancer, autoimmune disease, degeneration, physical/chemical/radiation injuries), how they heal or don't heal, and how they affect other beings around them as a herd (e.g. infectious and parasitic diseases).

As a scientist, I worked at academic and research institutions and the biopharmaceutical industry as an experimental and toxicologic pathologist to discover and develop new agents for various treatment areas (e.g. cancer, cardiovascular, autoimmune and metabolic diseases, etc.). The intention was to treat a disease condition, but as the early alchemists before us observed:

"All things are poison and nothing is without poison."
— Paracelsus (1493-1541)

After leaving the corporate world, I came across the work of Michael Newton, PhD ("Journey of Souls"), who pioneered the use of regression therapy to explore the soul's afterlife period in hundreds of people (below).

It was a game changer!

My worldview shifted from that of a left brained research scientist immersed in the physical world to that of a spiritual scientist curious about the nonphysical or energetic side of life, including near death experiences, astral projection, past lives, reincarnation, life between lives, and various channeled and esoteric teachings.

Eventually, my search for truth led me to Guy Needler's work. He has vastly expanded our understanding of who and what we are, our physical universe, multiverse and omniverse. He was an engineer prior to his schooling in various energy healing techniques. His eighth book ("Psycho-Spiritual Healing") explains how he heals people from the inside out — from the energetic side to the physical side — using both psycho-spiritual reprogramming and various energy and vibrational therapy techniques to heal the whole human being at once.

He has also given us a totally new perspective on poorly understood mental conditions, such as dementia, autism spectrum disorder, bipolar disorder, schizophrenia, attention deficit disorder, and obsessive compulsive disorder, as described in the previous chapters in this book.

How do drugs affect the body and soul? In Chapter 2 we learned that the human form is a very sophisticated vehicle, which is made of more than the 'flesh and bones' or the physical parts we can see. The human vehicle has several energetic templates and auric fields we can't see.

When we take prescription or recreational drugs, ALL these layers are affected in some way! That means drugs of any sort — whether they are uppers or downers, synthetic or natural, prescription or recreational drugs or even sacred plant medicines. While they may affect the healing process or mask an ailment, they also poison the physical vehicle.

"Any form of drug isn't good for us, not just from the physical perspective, but also from the energetic perspective and from the soul level." — Guy Needler

Needler said every drug affects our physicality. The drugs interfere with the energy flow, which lowers our frequency. Why? The **synthesized products** (i.e. chemicals created in the lab or scaled up by pharmaceutical manufacturing processes) are not really "pure."

It's not the same as taking the leaf of a plant and then crushing it all up and making some kind of "tincture" out of it that is infused with the plant's natural properties, and then making a drink out of it or spreading it on to a wound.

The synthetic chemical is diluted and taken away from what it is supposed to be. That level of dilution and 'mutation' creates a disproportionate and disharmonious frequency in the substance, which makes it incompatible to the body. As a result, the body fights it and in fighting it, it brings the frequencies of the body down. That's the energetic mechanism, according to Needler.

For example, the role of **pain killers** and **anesthetics** is to stop the function of the body in some way. A pain killer stops the sensory connectivity with the body and how it is transmitted back to the central nervous system. The anesthetic slows the body down to almost inanimation, so only the major organs are functioning.

From that perspective, it is inhibiting the soul's sentience (at the soul seat) and the animating energy (at the Tan tien) from interacting with the physical body, because it is so out of harmony (Chapter 2).

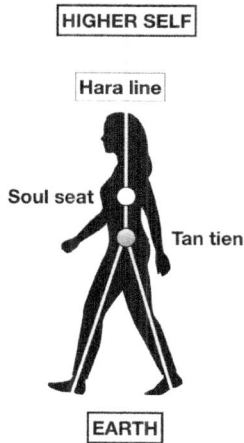

When the soul jumps out of the body, we get an *out of body experience* in the operating room. Most people don't remember it, which is why they don't report it. The soul gets out and the body goes to sleep and maintains a "tickover" state to run in a steady but slow way during anesthesia.

But every person is different. A particular drug may affect or damage one person more than another person, depending on their natural resistance to it both physically and energetically. The human form has a natural *lifespan*, which may be prolonged by natural ways (e.g. fasting, meditation, higher connectivity with Source) or by mechanical ways (e.g. surgery, medication).

All of us have *individualized free will* to decide what to do with ourselves. The choice to undergo therapy of any kind (or not) is personal, based on where our *life plan* is — whether we need to stay here to continue to learn, experience and evolve for our own sake or for the sake of others, who are supposed to interact with us at that stage or later in life. It's the soul's choice.

What are exit points? Most people find it hard to believe that our births and deaths are carefully orchestrated events. There are no such things as accidents. The soul leaves exactly when it wants to, and when it doesn't have anything else to accomplish in that lifetime or setting (see "Spiritual Guide To Our Afterlife").

The soul has *pre-planned* the manner of death and the timing of death at 3-5 exit points, according to Guy Needler ("The Anne Dialogues"). The decision to leave is made by the *soul* on the energetic level, not by the ego on the human level. The soul can leave at these exit points without incurring any karma. Why?

Because the exit was pre-planned with the other souls in that life, so that all their interactions from that point on come to a natural end. This is very different from **suicide**, which is not a planned event.

It creates a lot of unfinished business. It throws everybody else's life plans out the window, creating an evolutionary debt to all those other souls affected by the unplanned death. They were supposed to learn more about themselves and others through their downstream interactions with the person who died by suicide.

The exit points are spread out over our lifetime.

195

For example, the first exit point may be planned for when we are still in the womb (e.g. miscarriage, spontaneous abortion, stillbirth) or a baby (e.g. crib death) or a child (e.g. death at 0-7 years). The second exit point may occur at the ages of 8-21 years. The third exit point may be between 22-42 years, and the fourth one from midlife to 70 years of age. There is one more potential exit point before our body's natural death (beyond age 70+).

Every time we bypass one of these exit points, they "expire," so to speak. Then we move towards the next exit point. If we bypass all of these exit points, then we have to live out until the end of life as planned.

In hindsight, most of us recognize some events in our lives that could have been potential exit points (e.g. car accident, surgical complication, stroke, near drowning, being shot, organ failure, sudden life-threatening illness, etc.) that our soul chose not to take in order to experience, learn and evolve a bit longer in this body and setting.

On the other hand, some people may recognize an exit point (whether consciously or not) and refuse further treatment. For example, Albert Einstein (at 76) had an aortic aneurysm that burst in his abdomen. He went to the hospital, but refused further medical attention stating:

"I want to go when I want. It is tasteless to prolong life artificially. I have done my share, it is time to go. I will do it elegantly." — *Albert Einstein (1879-1955)*

How do recreational drugs affect the soul? A mind-altering (psychoactive, psychotropic) drug is any natural or synthetic chemical substance that changes brain function and alters perception, mood, or conscious-ness. There are many classes of drugs, which affect the central nervous system both physically and energetically, including CNS depressants (e.g. alcohol, heroin, oxycontin, valium), CNS stimulants (e.g. cocaine, methamphetamine), hallucinogens (e.g. LSD, psilocybin, peyote, ecstasy, ayahuasca) or dissociative hallucinogens (e.g. ketamine).

All these agents, whether natural or synthesized, are a *mechanical* way to achieve a greater level of *connectivity* to higher frequencies — they do it by throwing the soul out of the body. From the soul's perspective, the body is so disharmonious that the soul cannot stay within the energies associated with the gross physical body (FB 1-3) or even the astral bodies (FB 4-7).

The aura is a natural protective energetic shield around the body, which is enhanced by meditation, but altered or damaged by chronic drug abuse (image analogy, below).

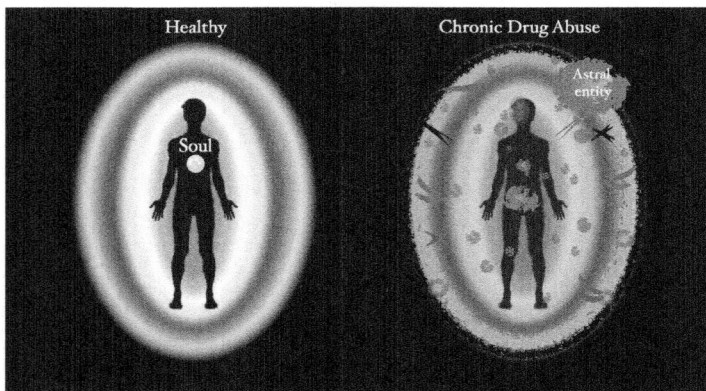

When the soul ejects itself out of body, the auric layers split open and the soul lands in the energy layers above the physical body. The problem is that damages the auric layers. They can become dull and dingy with holes, tears and dirt (above). The more drugs are taken, the more disharmonious the body becomes, and the higher the soul gets thrown.

A so-called "**good trip**" with psychedelics is where the soul is thrown to the upper astral levels (FB 6-7) with "heavenly" or timeless landscapes (below). The entities at these levels are higher frequency, so they are naturally more benign, loving and gracious. Since they are invisible to us, they don't need to scare us with any images.

A "**bad trip**" is where the soul is thrown to the lower astral levels (FB 4-5), where the soul has a lucid experience of the environments and astral entities that may be less benign. They search our memories for things that we are scared of and create an image based on whatever scares us (e.g. snakes, ghosts). That's why everybody's experience is a bit different (below).

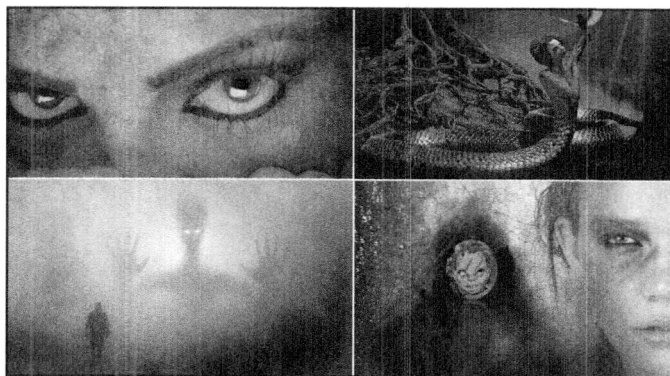

What's the problem with drugs? There are several things to consider here. When the soul's protection by the auric layers is reduced, the person becomes vulnerable to **attachment** by *astral entities* and *thought-forms* that take energy from the person, because they don't have their own way to metabolize energy (see "Spiritual Guide To Our Afterlife").

It takes three days to heal the auric layers, while the person is "**detoxing**" himself from a single drug exposure. That leaves all the energetic bodies vulnerable to astral attachment. The soul cannot come back to take charge of the body until the effects of the drugs wear off. But the person may have a hangover with headaches, lack of clear thinking or disturbing visualizations.

Over time, some people can develop **tolerance** to the drugs, so they need to take even higher doses or a combination of drugs to try to recreate the transcendent experience or the memory of it. Some people die from a **drug overdose**, while seeking a higher high. It can easily become a habit or a crutch, an attachment or addiction that leads to a downward spiral in life (Chapter 9).

Are drugs necessary for mystical experiences? Natural and synthetic mind-altering drugs have been used by people for millennia. But all these agents are a *mechanical way* to gain *temporary access* to an expanded perspective, according to Wendy Kennedy ("The Great Human Potential"). She said any mind-altering drug is mind originated.

Your 3D mind (like your body) is something you have, but it's not who you are. The mind was set up as a filter to allow us to have a limited perspective of reality.

Some people may use drugs as an excuse to numb themselves or not feel or perceive things in the same way.

For example, psilocybin (in "mushrooms") is like a sledgehammer that throws you into a state of selflessness, because it deactivates the brain regions (called default mode network) that deal with thinking about yourself, according to neuroscientist Judson Brewer, MD, PhD.

Since taking mind-altering drugs is a purely mechanical way to "get high," you're not really in charge, the drugs are. They may give you a transient glimpse at the energetic realms, but we don't really "own" the experience. Thus, it's not a shortcut to enlightenment, because it doesn't last. They may serve as a stepping stone, a "peek experience" or a window into the nonphysical or energetic realms or higher states, but they don't really serve you in the long term. Why?

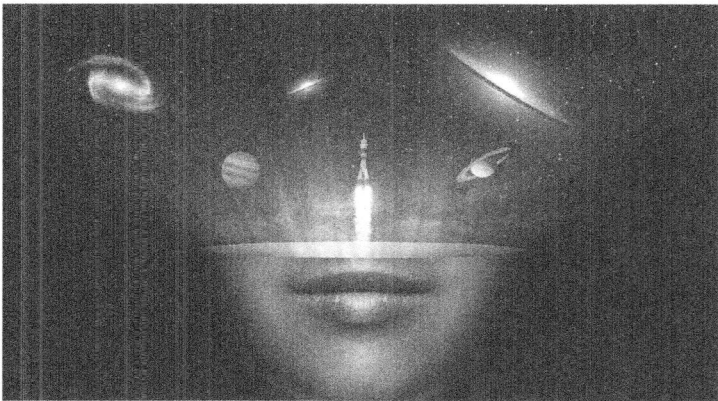

Psychoactive drugs can cause physical or psychological **dependence** and become a habit or a crutch. They can become a **distraction** or a **detour** from your life plan that was designed to interface with many other souls and learn about certain goals and challenges.

Some souls came here to experience something difficult, like **addiction**, so they could experience it, and then choose to move away from it. When the soul is able to *overcome* something difficult in life, it makes their Higher Self evolve faster.

Drugs can also become a form of **spiritual bypassing,** if used to avoid facing our shadows. We can't jump from shadows to higher frequencies without doing the inner work on ourselves. We incarnated here to experience, learn and evolve from facing, resolving and healing certain emotional issues, psychological wounds and needs. We need to be *grounded* to do that and to fulfill our obligations in the physical world.

Note: There is some evidence that certain mental conditions (e.g. heroin addiction, nicotine addiction, post-traumatic stress disorder, obsessive compulsive disorder, severe depression, anxiety, eating disorders, etc.) may respond to a single dose or microdosing of a mind-altering medication under supervision (e.g. ayahuasca, psilocybin, ketamine associated psychotherapy).

What is the best way to progress? When Guy Needler was asked if he personally took or advocated taking drugs for spiritual development, he said no.

"I've always had an innate feeling that we can do what we want to do by pure meditation, so the answer to that question is no, I've never had the desire. I don't advocate it. I don't think it's appropriate. It's unnecessary as well. It's a mechanical short cut, which ultimately results in us struggling to do it properly." — Guy Needler

The natural way forwards is **meditation**. When 3 to 4-year-old kids are taught to meditate, their third eye stays open, so they don't become "head blind" like most people. But we can start meditating at any age. There are many types of meditation techniques, all of which are helpful in our stressful lives. Meditation starts with relaxation techniques and goes deeper with practice.

Neuroscientists say we spend about half of our waking hours just thinking about ourselves, but meditation puts a damper on that. We go beyond identifying with our self all the time, whether it's for a few minutes or an hour or longer. We can meditate while sitting or lying down, walking or listening to music, praying or contemplating. Our focus can be on the breath, a mantra, visual imagery, sensations, chakras, or attitudes of love, peace, harmony, unity, etc.

We can do meditation on our own or in groups. When we do a group meditation, the energies are *amplified exponentially* based on the number of people present. That makes a huge difference. Imagine the power of a group meditation for peace and goodwill on our planet (below).

It's easier to connect to higher frequencies in a group. You can do it whether you are physically present or not. The "event space" is set up for you to join it energetically at any time.

When we learn to communicate with our Higher Self, which is located outside of the physical universe, while we're in human form, we're *self-realized*. We have **Christ consciousness**. When we can contact our Source at will, we're *God-realized* and have **Cosmic consciousness**. That's the goal — not some drug-induced astral trips at the bottom of this universe. We can do better!

Since we have a natural built-in energy system in our bodies, we can learn to project our consciousness or sentience to ANY level in this multiverse. One of the easiest ways to get started is to practice the **Chakra Opening Exercise** given by Guy Needler (see Appendix).

It exposes your body and sentience to frequencies above the gross physical level. It lifts your frequencies higher and keeps you there longer than any drug will, because *you* are in charge. It's a free, safe, robust and repeatable way to get a sense of expansion into Oneness.

"There is no limit to the extent of human consciousness. It can expand to fill the universe and then...you have a diplomatic visa to infinity." — *Itzhak Bentov*

Does that mean we should not take any drugs at all?
We know that many people rely on prescription drugs to help them deal with serious mental conditions (e.g. schizophrenia, bipolar disorder, obsessive compulsive disorder, attention deficit disorder, etc.). We also know that these conditions are seriously misunderstood, as described in the previous chapters.

Guy Needler said the use of drugs doesn't actually do anything. The medication slows them down, sedates them and creates disharmony, which reduces the sensitivity of the individual to the point where they can't connect to higher frequencies and the discarnate/incarnate entities at those levels. It seems to be a solution to a problem that they don't understand. When you remove those drugs and the body starts to go back up to the right frequency again, the person starts to get connected with those other entities again.

He said it's not a case of medicating them to eradicate the condition, it's a case of *educating* them (while they are under medication) to work with what they've got — a higher level of connectivity due to being a higher frequency human. They should be educated as to what these different entities are, where they might come from, and whether they're astral entities or whether they're higher frequency incarnate entities or whether they're disincarnate entities or whether there's another soul in their body or whether they're walk-ins, and so on.

Once they're educated and you can explain how they can deal with it — they can turn it off, they can turn it on, if they wanted to work with it. Once they're educated, then you can start to reduce the medication and keep an eye on them to see how well they do in their own interaction with these things and their own level of self-control.

Then we will find out that there's no need for the medication really, because these individuals now understand what's going on, and we understand what's going on, so it's not bizarre to us or classified as a problem. Then they can live a normal life knowing that they've got a different level of functionality. We accept that functionality rather than categorize it as being a psychosis of some sort or a "mental illness."

Who is in charge of the body? Our souls come here to experience "being human" with all the challenges and delights that come with it. When a soul is "fully immersed" in the human experience, the ego takes over the incarnation. The ego has command and control over the sentience, while the soul is more of an "observer" unless it becomes activated.

The problem is the ego thinks it IS the human body and nothing else. That's why we start to fear death — that's the ego talking, not the soul that knows it is eternal beyond form and time. But the ego is not a mistake either. We all have it and need it to anchor us to this linear reality.

The ego is made from a series of *programs* and *limiting filters* in our mind that create the human personality (the "you" here). These filters and programs keep us feeling small, limited, separate, abandoned, fearful, reactive, defensive or less than who and what we really are.

Our souls are master creators! The soul is what creates, energizes and animates the human form with all its layers as a vehicle to experience life on Earth. Wendy Kennedy said that we have enough soul energy to create a physical body in one reality right now, but eventually, we will be able to split the body's energy and *bilocate* into two places at once! Wow!

How do we balance western medicine and energy medicine? When we get sick, we tend to focus on the physical body and aren't aware of anything else. In western allopathic medicine we try to treat or cure a physical illness using various physical means, such as medicine, surgery, etc.

Over the years, the practice of medicine and surgery has become so specialized that it fails to treat the whole person or even understand the body as a highly interconnected whole system. Patients get referred from one doctor to another in a sickcare system where the left hand doesn't know what the right hand is doing. Most patients don't know any better and trust their doctors.

The result is *overdiagnosis* and *overmedication*, where 70% of Americans take at least one medication and 40% of older Americans take five or more medications. This may lead to adverse drug reactions, because multiple drug combinations have never been tested by the drug makers.

We treat mental illness the same way using medication, hospitalization, psychotherapy, etc. We talk about body/mind psychotherapy, biofeedback, breathwork, movement therapy, emotional freedom technique, etc., but we don't really understand the root of the problem — not in terms of its energetic or soul based origin. Most of us have no clue about the energetic origin of diseases or how to treat them.

As Wendy Kennedy ("The Great Human Potential") observed:

"For the most part, your allopathic medicine is just working with the physical, and it's only a temporary solution. This is why so many people will have recurring health issues.

*"**Ultimately, every issue you have is an energetic one without exception.** The solution to everything is energetic. If you don't change the energetic template by owning the thoughts and emotions that create the frequency for the body, you are not going to be able to permanently change the physical body." – Wendy Kennedy*

Nora Herold said we are not yet evolved beyond the point of pain and suffering on our world. It is still present in our "3D" experience of medicine, surgery and dentistry. Sometimes we hurt ourselves physically (e.g. twisted ankle), so that we can give ourselves an understanding of pain and deeper healing associated with a trauma that goes back to our childhood or past life (e.g. amputation or surgical procedures without anesthesia) or future life experiences that we wish to heal in this lifetime. Sometimes we experience a physical shift, like a "rewiring" after we heal.

She noted that often there is too much rejection of western medicine or science in the New Age or spiritual communities. You cannot reject it when you are trying to reunify science and spirituality. Sometimes we have a fear of being diagnosed due to "magical thinking," where we think hearing something about yourself will make it real. If it's a physical issue, it's already real, so thinking that it's not real is a bit of "spiritual bypassing" or trying to avoid it.

According to Herold, we may choose western medicine to help us work with the physical side until we're able to shift ourselves energetically. But we need to be willing to **take responsibility for our own health and well-being.**

Since we exist in physical bodies, sometimes we may need western medicine, while other times we may benefit from energy medicine. There is room for both approaches at our level of existence.

What is my guidance? Here is the guidance I got in channeling about my **health issues**:

"Listen to your body — it will tell you what it needs, what is going well (or not). Listen to your hunches and intuition as to what to do (e.g. meditate or medicate, undergo a surgical procedure, take supplements to restore function, use other "permission slips" to help you heal). You have overcome many physical issues already in this life.

Know that you need not play out physical diseases or conditions that you have learned to reverse by other means** — some by physical, dietary, lifestyle, energetic, or psycho-spiritual means — all these are new ways of dealing with diseases. **That is the lesson in this lifetime.

You are learning to work with your body on your own — to be the master manifestor or creator entity in training using the body as your mold, your sculpture, your medium.

Think of it in those terms and then you won't see anything as a life/death sentence, but rather as an opportunity to tweak this and that, like a tune up — not throwing everything out the window or shoving everything into your body as a remedy.

As Karen Curry put it, all this has to come from a place of nurturing, not from a place of fear.

You were given a body to enjoy it, to do things with it, to take care of it with proper food, proper exercise, proper care and hygiene energetically and physically. Don't get too wrapped up in the physical side of things. They will be healed, nurtured and helped with your energetic work — as a result of it, not because you need to do everything on the physical plane.

Connecting to your own soul, Higher Self, guide, and Source are the best medicine for all *people, if they would just do it. You are meant to come from a place of self-empowerment.*

As more people become aware of how they are creating their own health status by what they "feed it" in terms of physical food, mind-based food, like TV programs, movies and social media and such — all those things can be considered "food" or nourishment or like poison for the mind, emotional, etheric body and physical body — people will become more mindful of what is being fed to them, and what they choose to ingest in terms of these layers of beingness they inhabit." — Source (via Ulla)

Can we heal ourselves? Guy Needler said that the human form was supposed to be self-contained and self-maintained. We used to be able to heal ourselves and continue our existence as long as possible. But we've lost that ability, as we moved down the frequencies.

"We can tell our body to heal itself in any way, shape or form and it will do it, but only if we are in total synchronicity with the FACT that we are being healed. There can be no doubt." – Guy Needler

He said when we have a moment of doubt, the initiative or the incentive or the action is gone from the **desire to**

heal or be healed. We are being coerced into believing that we need to have a constant stream of *medication* to keep us alive, but actually we don't. We need a constant stream of *meditation* to keep us alive. In addition, energy healing may be used to heal specific issues.

His **energy healing techniques** include chelation or basic energy balancing, reconstruction of chakras, organs, body parts or energy templates, past life trauma healing, psychic surgery, astral entity removal, astral mucus clearing, virus clearing, spine cleansing, brain balancing and clearing, Hara line realignment, removing karmic links, removing foreign objects from the auric layers and energetic templates, removing non-karmic links with other incarnates, psychological issues associated with higher frequency incarnation (e.g. ADHD, bipolarism, etc.), walk-ins, healing uncontrolled event space interaction, psycho-spiritual reprogramming, and more.

There is no "one-size-fits-all" healing method. Energy healing at the psychological, energetic and spiritual levels usually requires several years of specialized training (e.g. Barbara Brennan School of Healing, Guy Needler's Healing Workshops) and access to higher intuitive functions that can be used to "see" or "know" the issues affecting the person at all levels of their gross physical and subtle energetic bodies. That's the starting point for shifting their condition.

How do we shift realities? Before we can talk about "miraculous" healing, we need learn how we shift realities. Guy Needler and others have told us that there is no such thing as "**time**." Time is invented by humans to view things as a finite series of events in *linear time.* But time doesn't really exist except in our *minds.*

We exist in **event space** where all events happen in the same space at the same time. That means our past, present and future are **event points** that create the *illusion* of time. Time is just a marker for an event potential in spherical event space. Different things occupy different layers of that space based on their frequencies (below).

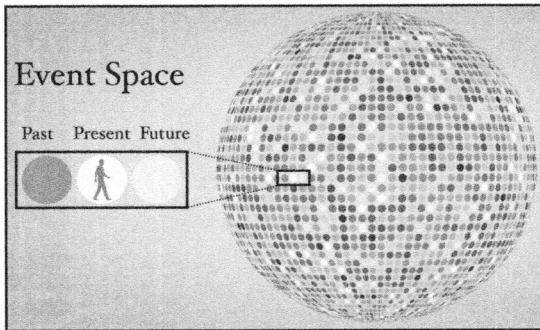

Event Space

Past   Present   Future

Our reality is based on which event point we *choose* to focus our consciousness on. That becomes our "present" moment. We're constantly moving from one event point (now moment) to another to create a "timeline" or an **event stream**. All these event points are slightly different from each other. Each has a specific set of circumstances for us to experience.

For example, here is a snowboarder in three different event points — first taking off, then sliding down the hill and then coming to a stop (below). That's one event stream.

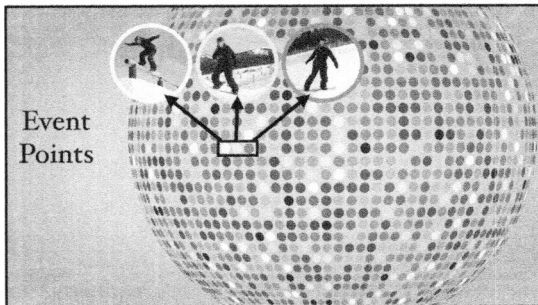

Event Points

Here is the same snowboarder shown in a different event stream, where the guy falls down and breaks his ankle (below). That was the expected direction of events in *that* event stream or "timeline."

You can see that there are numerous potential events for us to experience. Why? Because everything that has already happened and will ever happen is happening right now, meaning simultaneously. All realities are already in existence in that sphere of event space. But they are like hollow shells that are *not "enlivened"* until **we** put our spark into them and play with them.

That means if something is happening to you now, it's because you're supposed to be experiencing it now, even if it's a broken ankle! It's not your fault. It's just an event that your soul thought would serve you in some way, because it shows you something about yourself or allows you to serve someone else or the collective. There is nothing wrong with you per se.

You are experiencing it, but you are not that experience. It also doesn't mean that everything is predestined or *fated* to happen to you. When we interact with these possibilities as *co-creators,* we can add and subtract and modify these realities. Then they will be in place for those who come after us, and they can play with them as they wish, according to Guy Needler. None of us are going over old ground in that sense.

What is a miracle? Wendy Kennedy ("The Great Human Potential") said that the point we are standing on is **based on the stories** we tell ourselves (e.g. this is who I am, these are the things that happened to me, etc.). That creates the *base frequency* for that point, but we can choose another point (e.g. jump from event point A to a higher frequency event point B, below).

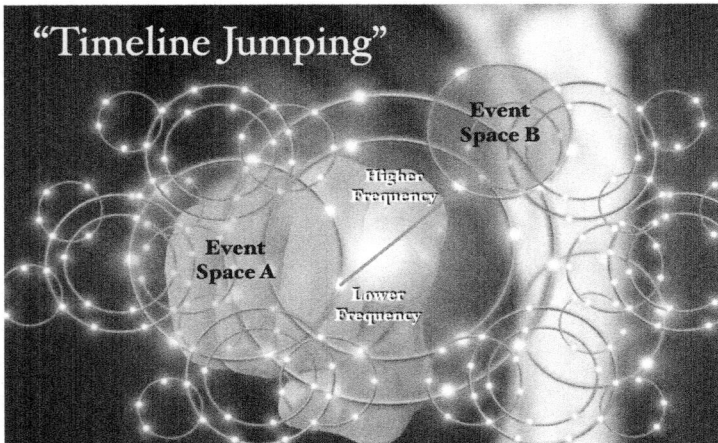

What we consider to be a "**miracle**" is when we shift to another event point, where the base frequency is dramatically different from the one we were standing on.

Typically, the **soul** wants to keep the points pretty close, so it doesn't disrupt the game we're playing. But the soul could jump to another point that is vastly different (e.g. WWII didn't happen, your parents didn't get divorced, your breast cancer or car accident or broken leg didn't happen or other potentials).

When it comes to a health issue, we can tell ourselves a different story. We can change our perspective of reality.

For example, instead of being in a lot of pain and feeling victimized about it, because somebody did something to you, you can realign yourself, forgive the other person, so you are at peace with it and perceive yourself as a co-creator of the situation.

The **new story** shifts you to another point, where the base frequency is higher. The pain goes away in an instant, because you have shifted your energetic template. It's not a matter of time — **it's a matter of belief**. But since we still operate under the belief system of "linear time," some time may be required to make the shift, according to Kennedy.

We need to remember that by changing the base frequency alone, **we can create a completely different reality** for ourselves both individually and collectively (see "Spiritual Guide To Our Multiverse").

What's the point? We are NOT our body or mind or soul or experience. We are more than all those put together. The body is a vehicle that the soul drives around for a while. The *soul* chooses which realities to explore as **parallel selves** in the human form you have. Why?

Because evolution is *experiential*, according to Guy Needler. It's getting a full understanding from every angle. That means your soul might want to explore smoking and drinking as a young man, for instance.

Do you get lung cancer and die early? Or do you stop smoking and start taking care of your health? Do you become addicted to alcohol? Or do you overcome that addiction? These are the kinds of parallel experiences that the soul may choose to explore in some lifetimes.

Ram Dass ("Polishing the Mirror") wrote about illness in his 80s stating:

"Before my stroke, I was on a very spiritual plane. I ignored my body, took it for granted. I wanted to be free of the physical plane, the psychological plane, and when I got free of those, the stroke reminded me that I had a body and a brain that I had to honor.

These days I see myself as a soul who has taken incarnation in a body that suffered a stroke. So while my ego thought I was a person with a stroke, that suffering pushed me into my soul, which witnesses or watches the incarnation." — *Ram Dass (1931-2019)*

He realized that he was in this incarnation to learn about his soul. Along the way he also learned about strokes, broken hips and pain throughout his body. But he didn't identify with the pains he listed for his doctors. He identified with being a witness of pain — not as the pain, but living with the pain, as a vehicle for *awakening*.

At this time on Earth, we may need physical help (via western medicine) and spiritual or energetic help (via energy medicine) to heal ourselves. But we also need to move away from the *old spiritual paradigm*, where we believe we can only grow through *suffering*. No pain, no gain?

We have accepted suffering as part of our reality after many lives that had suffering, as noted by Nora Herold. Now we need to disconnect from the idea that it is needed or beneficial to us. Why? You don't grow from pain and suffering, you shrink, contract and get stuck in suffering.

Enough already! It's time to *re-write* our personal and collective stories about how we grow.

In the new spiritual paradigm, we grow through healing. We are using healing as a very *conscious tool* on our journey to manifestation and creation, as noted by Nora Herold. Clear and release the outdated beliefs of pain and suffering to make room for Love and Joy instead!

What lights you up? What feels good? Do more of that — find more moments of joy, fun, play, creation, love, appreciation and gratitude. Then watch the "miracles" show up in your life, as you shift your reality from one joyful moment to another again and again and again...Smile! You got this!

"You are Love incarnate. Operate from JOY." — *Nora Herold*

"There are two ways to live your life. One is as though nothing is a miracle. The other is as though everything is a miracle." — *Albert Einstein*

BIBLIOGRAPHY

Ulla Sarmiento: Spiritual Guide To Our Multiverse, 2018

Ulla Sarmiento: Guía Espiritual a Nuestro Multiverso, 2018

Ulla Sarmiento: Spiritual Guide To Our Afterlife, 2019

Ulla Sarmiento: Spiritual Guide To Our Relationships, 2020

Ulla Sarmiento: Spiritual Guide To Our Universal Laws, 2021

Ulla Sarmiento: Spiritual Guide To Our Awakening, 2021

My website: BigPictureQuestions(dot)com

My YouTube Channel: Ulla Sarmiento - YouTube

Guy Needler: The History of God, 2011

Guy Needler: Beyond the Source, Book 1, 2012

Guy Needler: Beyond the Source, Book 2, 2013

Guy Needler: Avoiding Karma, 2014

Guy Needler: The Origin Speaks, 2015

Guy Needler: The Anne Dialogues, 2016

Guy Needler: The Curators, 2019

Guy Needler: Psycho-Spiritual Healing, 2021

Guy Needler: BeyondtheSource(dot)org (website)

Anodea Judith: Eastern Body, Western Mind, 2004

Anodea Judith: Charge and the Energy Body, 2018

Richard Barrett: A New Psychology of Human Well-Being, 2016

Barbara Brennan: Hands of Light, 1987

Cyndi Dale: The Subtle Body, 2009

Louise Hay: You Can Heal Your Life, 1984

Wilhelm Reich: Character Analysis, 1939

Lucia Aronica: draronica(dot)com (website)

Wendy Kennedy: HigherFrequencies(dot)net (website)

Tom Kenyon & Wendy Kennedy: The Great Human Potential, 2013

Nora Herold: NoraHerold(dot)com (website)

Ra Uru Hu: The Complete Rave I'Ching, 2001

Lynda Bunnell & Ra Uru Hu: Human Design, 2011

Karen Curry: Understanding Human Design, 2013

Richard Rudd: Gene Keys, 2009

Chetan Parkyn: The Book of Lines, 2012

Jason Fung: The Obesity Code, 2016

Jason Fung: The Diabetes Code, 2018

Juan Sarmiento: FeastFastForLife(dot)com (website) & Juan Sarmiento - YouTube

Dale Bredesen: The End of Alzheimers, 2017

Mark D. White: PsychologyToday(dot)com/ DepressionCenter (website)

John Bradshaw: The Family, 1988

Gordon Phinn: You Are History, 2015

John Welwood: Perfect Love, Imperfect Relationships, 2005

Dolores Cannon: The Three Waves of Volunteers, 2012

Michael Newton: The Journey of Souls, 1994

Michael Newton: The Destiny of Souls, 2000

Michael Newton: Life Between Lives, 2004

Ram Dass: Polishing the Mirror, 2014

Neale Donald Walsch: The Complete Conversations with God, 2005

Itzhak Bentov: A Brief Tour of Higher Consciousness, 2000

Aaron Christeaan, JP Van Hulle & MC Clark: Michael: The Basic Teachings, 1990

Peter Watson Jenkins & Toni Ann Winninger: Talking With Twentieth-Century Women, 2008

Doris E Cohen: Repetition: Past Lives, Life, and Rebirth, 2008

José Stevens & Simon Warwick-Smith: The Michael Handbook, 1990

Emily Matweow: Meet the Clairs, OKinHealth(dot)com & emily(dot)org (website)

Deborah Kaplan: Independent Living Articles (jik(dot)com/ ilarts)

Lissa Rankin: LissaRankin(dot)com (website)

Shelley Young: TrinityEsoterics(dot)com (website)

Susann Taylor Shier: SoulMastery(dot)net (website)

Gin S Malhi et al.: The 2020 clinical practice guidelines for mood disorders, ANZJP 55(1), 2021

Carrie Brown: Putting bipolar 2 disorder into remission (see DietDoctor(dot)com)

Sethi Dalai: Metabolic Psychiatry Clinic (for obesity, schizophrenia, bipolar disorder)

KM Antshel et al.: Advanced in understanding and treating ADHD, BMC Medicine 9: 72, 2011

Images: All figures and photographs used in the text are in the public domain or obtained as free images from Pixabay or created by the author.

Disclaimer: The health and medical information in this book is provided as an information resource only, and is not to be used or relied on for any diagnostic or treatment purposes. Please consult your health care provider before making any health care decisions about your condition.

APPENDIX

Chakra Opening Exercise by Guy Steven Needler (reprinted with permission from his website — beyondthesource.org):

Original Audio (mp3) link: http://www.beyondthesource.org/chakra-opening-exercises-audio/ (about 27 min)

Original Written (PDF) link: http://www.beyondthesource.org/wp-content/uploads/2015/02/Chakra-Opening-Exercises-1.pdf

Here is a powerful **Chakra Opening Exercise** that can be used to energize the body. Guy Needler teaches this as a prelude to his "Traversing the Frequencies" workshops. This exercise allows everybody to have a first-hand experience of being more than their gross physical human body.

This is a short meditation, which is fairly simple to do either when you go to bed at night or when you wake up in the morning. You can do this to energize yourself and raise your frequencies. The meditation is based upon the chakra opening exercises because opening the chakras energizes the body on all levels.

1. **Find a quiet room** where you will not be disturbed.

2. **Stand** with your knees slightly bent, feet shoulder width apart, arms and hands by your side, close your eyes and focus on the area of the third eye, the spiritual eye which is positioned above the bridge of the nose and between the eye brows. (**You can sit in a straight backed chair**, if you prefer).

3. **Ground yourself** by imagining a climber's rope attached to you and an anchor buried deeply in the ground. You will need this, and you should keep referring to this grounding link throughout this exercise. This will help you return to the physical.

4. **Concentrate on your base chakra** [root, above]. Imagine it as a cone and extend it vertically downwards out to its full extension of 9"-12". Then rotate it clockwise. To assist you in the correct rotation imagine you have a clock on the floor and that your Chakra rotation is mirroring the second hand rotating from left to right. When a Chakra is fully extended and rotated in this way it effectively opens it allowing it to receive the energies necessary to invoke the **1st Auric layer – the etheric** allowing you to also assume this level. Feel the energies that being on this level, the etheric level, Level 1 gives you. Do you feel tingling, see colours or images in your closed eye vision, feel heat/cold, feel pressures around your head, experience emotional changes – these are all signs that your physical body is experiencing the energies associated with this level; they are proof of this change in frequency. Make a mental note of it.

5. **Move on to the second chakra,** the sacral. Imagine it as a cone and extend it horizontally in front of you, out to its full extension of 9"-12". Then rotate it clock-wise. To assist you in the correct rotation imagine you have a clock on a wall in front of you and that your Chakra rotation is mirroring the second hand rotating from left to right. When a Chakra is fully extended and rotated in this way it effectively opens it allowing it to receive the energies necessary to invoke the **2nd Auric layer – the Emotional layer** allowing us to also assume this level. Feel the energies that being on this level, emotional

level. Do you feel tingling, see colours or images in your closed eye vision, feel heat/cold, feel pressures around your head, experience emotional changes – these are all signs that your physical body is experiencing the energies associated with this level; they are proof of this change in frequency. What is the change in this level compared to that experienced in the previous level? Make a mental note of it.

6. **Move on to the third chakra,** the solar. Imagine it as a cone and extend it horizontally in front of you, out to its full extension of 9"-12". Then rotate it clock-wise. To assist you in the correct rotation imagine you have a clock on a wall in front of you and that your Chakra rotation is mirroring the second hand rotating from left to right. When a Chakra is fully extended and rotated in this way it effectively opens it allowing it to receive the energies necessary to invoke the **3rd Auric layer – the mental body** layer allowing us to also assume this level. Feel the energies that being on this level, mental body level. Do you feel tingling, see colours or images in your closed eye vision, feel heat/cold, feel pressures around your head, experience emotional changes – these are all signs that your physical body is experiencing the energies associated with this level; they are proof of this change in frequency. What is the change in this level compared to that experienced in the previous level? Make a mental note of it.

7. **Move on to the fourth chakra,** the heart. Imagine it as a cone and extend it horizontally in front of you, out to its full extension of 9"-12". Then rotate it clock-wise. To assist you in the correct rotation imagine you have a clock on a wall in front of you and that your Chakra rotation is mirroring the second hand rotating from left

to right. When a Chakra is fully extended and rotated in this way it effectively opens it allowing it to receive the energies necessary to invoke the **4th Auric layer – the astral layer** allowing us to also assume this level. Feel the energies that being on this level, astral level. Do you feel tingling, see colours or images in your closed eye vision, feel heat/cold, feel pressures around your head, experience emotional changes – these are all signs that your physical body is experiencing the energies associated with this level; they are proof of this change in frequency. What is the change in this level compared to that experienced in the previous level? Make a mental note of it.

8. **Move on to the fifth chakra,** the throat. Imagine it as a cone and extend it horizontally in front of you, out to its full extension of 9"-12". Then rotate it clock-wise. To assist you in the correct rotation imagine you have a clock on a wall in front of you and that your Chakra rotation is mirroring the second hand rotating from left to right. When a Chakra is fully extended and rotated in this way it effectively opens it allowing it to receive the energies necessary to invoke the **5th Auric layer – the etheric template** layer allowing us to also assume this level. Feel the energies that being on this level, etheric template level. Do you feel tingling – are they getting finer, see colours or images in your closed eye vision, feel heat/cold, feel pressures around your head, experience emotional changes – these are all signs that your physical body is experiencing the energies associated with this level; they are proof of this change in frequency. What is the change in this level compared to that experienced in the previous level? Make a mental note of it.

9. **Move on to the sixth chakra,** the third or spiritual eye. Imagine it as a cone and extend it horizontally in front of you, out to its full extension of 9"-12". Then rotate it clock-wise. To assist you in the correct rotation imagine you have a clock on a wall in front of you and that your Chakra rotation is mirroring the second hand rotating from left to right. When a Chakra is fully extended and rotated in this way it effectively opens it allowing it to receive the energies necessary to invoke the **6th Auric layer – the celestial body** layer allowing us to also assume this level. Feel the energies that being on this level, celestial body level. Do you feel tingling – are they getting still finer, see colours or images in your closed eye vision, feel heat/cold, feel pressures around your head, experience emotional changes – these are all signs that your physical body is experiencing the energies associated with this level; they are proof of this change in frequency. What is the change in this level compared to that experienced in the previous level? Make a mental note of it.\

10. **Finally move on to the seventh chakra,** the crown. Imagine it as a cone and extend it up towards the ceiling vertically out to its full extension of 9"-12". Then rotate it clock-wise. To assist you in the correct rotation imagine you have a clock on the ceiling above you and that your Chakra rotation is mirroring the second hand rotating from left to right. When a Chakra is fully extended and rotated in this way it effectively opens it allowing it to receive the energies necessary to invoke the **7th Auric layer – the ketheric template layer** allowing us to also assume this level. Feel the energies that being on this level, ketheric template level. Do you feel tingling – are they getting still finer or have they

gone, see colours or images in your closed eye vision, feel heat/cold, feel pressures around your head, experience emotional changes – these are all signs that your physical body is experiencing the energies associated with this level; they are proof of this change in frequency. What is the change in this level compared to that experienced in the previous level? Make a mental note of it. You are now at the end of the physicality/ spirituophysicality of your human form. Stay at this level of a few moments absorb how you feel, what your physical body has experienced, giving you proof, physical proof that you have actually risen above those frequencies that you are normally associated with on the earth level – the zero level.

11. **Slowly close each chakra one by one**, starting at the crown chakra and finishing with the Base Chakra by first stopping the rotation of the chakra and then withdrawing it back into its location of origin (refer to the section on chakra name, and location at the back of this lesson). Make a note of the feelings, the feel tingling – are they getting coarser as you descend the frequencies, colours or images in your closed eye vision, heat/cold, pressures around your head, emotional changes. The experiences, the responses that the human form gives you, should be repeated on each of the levels in the descent in reverse order of that which you experienced them on the ascent.

12. **To move down** from the seventh frequency level to the sixth frequency level stop the rotation of the crown chakra and withdraw it back into the crown area of the head. You are now on the sixth frequency level. To move down from the sixth frequency level to the fifth frequency level stop the rotation of the third eye chakra and withdraw it back into the area in-between the

eyebrows and above the bridge of the nose. You are now on the fifth frequency level. To move down from the fifth frequency level to the fourth frequency level stop the rotation of the throat eye chakra and withdraw it back into the area of the "Adam's apple". You are now on the fourth frequency level. To move down from the fourth frequency level to the third frequency level stop the rotation of the heart chakra and withdraw it back into the area in the centre of the sternum. You are now on the third frequency level.

13. To move down from the third frequency level to the second frequency level stop the rotation of the solar chakra and withdraw it back into the area 3 inches above the navel. You are now on the second frequency level. To move down from the second frequency level to the first frequency level stop the rotation of the sacral chakra and withdraw it back into the area 3 inches below the navel. You are now on the first frequency level. To move down from the first frequency level to the zero frequency level, the Earth level stop the rotation of the base chakra and withdraw it back up into the area of the groin. **You are now back on the zero frequency level, the Earth level.**

14. Finish by removing the mountaineering harness or belt and drinking some water to assist in the grounding."

15. You're done! You're now running much higher frequencies through your body than when you started. Enjoy the energies! Repeat this exercise daily to stay naturally "high" and self-empowered no matter what is happening in the outer world.

"Stay Light, Be Light, Light the way for others." – Guy Needler

For more meditations to heal yourself, repair your templates, organs or body parts, based on Guy Needler's psycho-spiritual healing techniques, please check out these posts at my website — BigPictureQuestions(dot)com:

How To Quickly Heal Your Body and Energetic Templates? - Big Picture Questions (http://bigpicturequestions.com/how-to-quickly-heal-your-body-and-energetic-templates/)

How To Energetically Repair Or Replace an Organ Or Body Part In Our Human Form? - Big Picture Questions (http://bigpicturequestions.com/how-to-energetically-repair-or-replace-an-organ-or-body-part-in-our-human-form/)

ABOUT THE AUTHOR

I consider myself a citizen of the world, since I was born in Finland, grew up in Canada, and lived in six different states in the United States. We now live in Spain.

I got my education in Canada, where I graduated as a veterinarian (DVM) and specialized in veterinary pathology (PhD). I became a board certified pathologist (ACVP) and taught at two veterinary schools before joining the pharmaceutical and biotechnology industries as an experimental pathologist to support drug discovery and drug development at two companies.

After retiring from the corporate world, I started researching spiritual science, which led to my blog (www.bigpicturequestions.com). I took Guy Needler's "Traversing the Frequencies" Workshops, learned to channel Source and Origin to work as a spiritual mentor and consultant.

My website has over 590+ articles on the Greater Reality, Incarnation, Health, Disease, Death, Afterlife, Love, Money, Karma, and Spiritual Topics. My primary goal is to bridge science and spirituality by bringing new ideas, thought processes and concepts into both areas to help us expand into the greater reality.

This is the sixth book in the "Big Picture Questions" Book Series, because there is so much new information to share. My first book was published in 2018 in both English ("Spiritual Guide To Our Multiverse") and Spanish versions ("Guía Espiritual a Nuestro Multiverso") available at Smashwords in all ebook formats and at Amazon in Kindle and Paperback formats.

My second book ("Spiritual Guide To Our Afterlife") was published in 2019. My third book ("Spiritual Guide To Our Relationships") was published in 2020. My fourth book ("Spiritual Guide To Our Universal Laws") and fifth book ("Spiritual Guide To Our Awakening") were published in 2021. There may be a couple of more books to come.

You can reach me through my website or by email: Ulla(at)bigpicturequestions(dot)com for more information or for personal life plan (or soul blueprint) readings and relationship readings.

"Have sentience, will travel." — *Ulla*

Printed in Great Britain
by Amazon